12-11-19 .50

A mouthful of breath mints and no one to kiss

Other "Cathy" books from Andrews and McMeel:

It Must Be Love. My Face Is Breaking Out

Another Saturday Night of Wild and Reckless Abandon

Cathy's Valentine's Day Survival Book

How to Get Rich, Fall in Love, Lose Weight, and Solve All Your Problems by Saying "No"

Eat Your Way to a Better Relationship

A mouthful of breath mints and no one to kiss

by Cathy Guisewite

Andrews and McMeel, Inc.
A Universal Press Syndicate Company
Kansas City • New York

A cathy® Collection

A Mouthful of Breath Mints and No One to Kiss copyright © 1983 by Universal Press Syndicate. All rights reserved. Printed in the United States of America. No part of this book may be used or reproduced in any manner whatsoever without written permission except in the case of reprints in the context of reviews. For information write Andrews and McMeel, Inc., a Universal Press Syndicate Company, 4400 Johnson Drive, Fairway, Kansas 66205.

ISBN: 0-8362-1120-0

Library of Congress Catalog Card Number: 83-71766

CATHY® is syndicated internationally by Universal Press Syndicate.

FIRST THERE WERE CARDS. THEN THERE WERE CARDS AND FLOWERS.
VALENTINES

THEN THERE WERE CARDS, FLOWERS AND CANDY. THEN THERE WERE CARDS, FLOWERS, CANDY AND JEWELRY.
VALENTINES

NOW THERE ARE CARDS, FLOWERS, CANDY, JEWELRY, TRINKET BOXES, BALLOONS, DESK ACCESSORIES, T-SHIRTS, UNDERWEAR, BOOKS, STICKERS AND SMALL APPLIANCES.
LOVE

EVERY YEAR THERE ARE MORE THINGS I'M NOT GOING TO GET FOR VALENTINE'S DAY.
LOVE
GUISEWITE

IRVING'S DOING IT TO ME, AGAIN, ANDREA. I CAN'T BELIEVE IT!

YAAAA! I'M SO MAD AT YOU, IRVING!

TAKE THAT! AND THAT! AND THAT!!
CATHY, WHY DON'T YOU JUST YELL AT IRVING INSTEAD OF BEATING UP ON YOUR LIVING ROOM?

I DIDN'T HAVE THE ENERGY TO GET INTO A BIG DISCUSSION.
GUISEWITE

DO YOU THINK I SHOULD SEND DAVID A VALENTINE?
YES, CATHY. DAVID SEEMS LIKE A NICE YOUNG MAN.

WHAT'S THE POINT IN PURSUING A RELATIONSHIP WITH A MAN WHO LIVES HUNDREDS OF MILES AWAY?
THEN, NO. DON'T SEND HIM A VALENTINE.

MOM, HE'S THE MOST UNDERSTANDING MAN I'VE EVER MET!
THEN, YES. BY ALL MEANS, SEND HIM A VALENTINE.

MY MOTHER IS INCAPABLE OF MAKING A DECISION.
GUISEWITE

PART OF ME DOESN'T EVEN CARE ABOUT VALENTINE'S DAY THIS YEAR... ANOTHER PART OF ME WANTS AN APARTMENT FULL OF CARDS AND FLOWERS...
VALENTINES
Be Mine
To my Darling
LOVE

PART OF ME THINKS VALENTINE'S DAY IS A CHEAP, COMMERCIALIZED EVENT... ANOTHER PART OF ME IS SCREAMING FOR PINK DOILIES AND POETRY...

PART OF ME DOESN'T NEED MY SELF-ESTEEM RAISED BY A VALENTINE... ANOTHER PART OF ME WOULD BEG AND GROVEL FOR ANYTHING WITH A HEART ON IT.

I'LL HAVE THE NACHOS FOR SIX.

QUICK! I ATE THE BOX OF CHOCOLATE MY BOYFRIEND GAVE ME FOR VALENTINE'S DAY AND I HAVE TO REPLACE IT BEFORE HE COMES OVER AND SEES THE EMPTY BOX!
½ price Valentines

QUICK! I ATE THE BOX OF CHOCOLATE I GOT TO REPLACE THE BOX MY BOYFRIEND GOT ME AND I HAVE TO REPLACE IT AGAIN!
½ price Valentines

QUICK! I ATE THE BOX OF CHOCOLATE I GOT TO REPLACE THE BOX THAT REPLACED THE BOX MY BOYFRIEND GAVE ME AND I NEED ANOTHER ONE!!
½ price Valentines

...SORRY I CAN'T MAKE IT OVER, CATHY. I HAVE TO GO OUT OF TOWN FOR A WEEK.

I MIGHT NOT GET A CHANCE TO CALL YOU FROM BOSTON, CATHY, BUT I'LL BE BACK NEXT WEEK. I LOVE YOU.
WHAT?

I'LL BE BACK NEXT WEEK. I LOVE YOU.
YOU WHAT? YOU LOVE ME? IRVING, WHERE ARE YOU?

I'M STANDING IN THE AIRPORT. OOPS. GOTTA GO. BYE.

WHY DON'T YOU EVER SAY YOU LOVE ME WHEN YOU'RE STANDING IN MY LIVING ROOM?!!

IRVING CALLED FROM THE AIRPORT. HE SAID HE LOVES ME.
HAH! MEN ONLY DO THAT SO YOU'LL FEEL TOO GUILTY TO GO OUT WITH ANYONE ELSE WHILE THEY'RE GONE!

IRVING CALLED FROM THE AIRPORT. HE SAID HE LOVES ME.
HAH! HE WAS JUST PRE-APOLOGIZING FOR ALL THE MISERABLE THINGS HE'S GOING TO DO ON HIS TRIP!

IRVING CALLED FROM THE AIRPORT. HE SAID HE LOVES ME.

GOOD FRIENDS KNOW WHEN TO KEEP THEIR MOUTHS SHUT.
Guisewite

I DISAGREE, MR. PINKLEY. MY RESEARCH INDICATES THAT OUR '82 GOALS WILL ONLY BE ACHIEVABLE IF WE PAY CA TION TO THE

I DISAGREE, MR. PINKLEY. MY RESEARCH INDICATES OUR '82 GOALS WILL BE ACHIEVABLE IF

INKLEY. ICATES OUR '82 GOALS WILL BE ACHIEVABLE IF

YOUR COMMENTS, CATHY?
THAT'S THE LAST TIME I PLAY PAC-MAN DURING LUNCH.
PRODUCT TESTING
Guisewite

NOT AGAIN... HOW AM I SUPPOSED TO GET ANY WORK DONE IF I'M ANSWERING CALLS ALL DAY??
RING RING
CATHY

SHUT UP! JUST SHUT UP!!
RING
RING RING
RING
RING
RING RING

CATHY, YOUR PHONE'S BEEN BUSY FOR HOURS!

SORRY, MR. PINKLEY. IT MUST HAVE SLIPPED OFF THE HOOK.
CATHY
Guisewite

WILL THERE BE ANY PROBLEM GETTING REFILLS FOR THIS PHOTO ALBUM?
GOODNESS NO.
ALBUMS
Photo Photo Phot
Photo Album

THEY'VE BEEN MAKING THESE FOR YEARS.
GREAT. I HATE BUYING SOMETHING AND THEN NOT BEING ABLE TO FIND REFILLS FOR IT.

NO PROBLEM. THAT KIND WILL BE AROUND FOREVER!
THANK YOU VERY MUCH.

YOU CAN STOP PRODUCTION ON THOSE REFILLS NOW.
Guisewite

ATTENTION ALL EMPLOYEES: IN HONOR OF MR. PINKLEY'S BIRTHDAY...
PRODUCT TESTING —INC.—
RECEPTIONIST

...THERE USED TO BE A CAKE IN THE COFFEE ROOM.
PRODUCT TESTING —INC.—
RECEPTIONIST
Guisewite

I THOUGHT YOU SAID IRVING LOVED THAT DRESS, CATHY.
SOMETIMES PEOPLE SAY THEY LOVE SOMETHING WHEN IT'S HIDEOUS AND THEY DON'T WANT TO HURT YOUR FEELINGS.

SOMETIMES THEY SAY THEY LOVE SOMETHING JUST TO AVOID COMMENTING ON HOW FAT YOU'VE GOTTEN. SOMETIMES THEY SAY IT WHEN THEY WANT TO BREAK UP AND THEY'RE STALLING FOR TIME.

HOW DOES IRVING FEEL ABOUT THAT DRESS?
HE HATES THIS ONE.

BUT AT LEAST I WON'T HAVE TO WONDER WHAT HE'S THINKING.
Guisewite

IRVING! WELCOME BACK! I MISSED YOU SO MUCH!
CATHY! YOU'RE HERE!
GATE 72
TO PLANE

IRVING, PRECIOUS... WOULD YOU MIND DRIVING A TOUCH SLOWER? THE ROADS ARE SO SLIPPERY.
I HAVE IT UNDER CONTROL, HONEY.

IRVING MY DARLING, IF YOU DO NOT SLOW DOWN I AM GOING TO JUMP OUT OF THE CAR AND WALK HOME!!
I AM AN EXCELLENT DRIVER, SWEETHEART!!

JUST ONCE I WISH A RELATIONSHIP WOULD LAST ALL THE WAY HOME FROM THE AIRPORT.

YOU KNOW WHAT'S WRONG WITH RELATIONSHIPS, ANDREA?... KITCHENS!

WHO COOKS... WHO CLEANS UP... THESE MEANINGLESS QUESTIONS UNDERMINE THE BEST OF ROMANCES.

IT'S A RELIEF TO GO TO THE OFFICE WHERE NO ONE CARES ABOUT WHAT HAPPENS IN THE STUPID KITCHEN!!!

ON THE TOP OF OUR AGENDA TODAY IS "KITCHEN DUTY."

YAAAK! JUST A SECOND! OKAY! WAIT! YAAACK! OKAY, OKAY, JUST A SECOND! WAIT!!
PICK UP LINE ONE
RING RING

COME ON, CATHY. IT'S AFTER 6:30.
RING RING

IT LOOKS LIKE A LITTLE ANGEL WHEN IT'S SLEEPING.

CHEESECAKE...FUDGE RIPPLE... CHOCOLATE ECLAIRS...COOKIES...
COOKIES
FUDGE RIPPLE

DIET POP! DIET SALAD DRESSING! DIET FROZEN DINNERS!

CHECK OUT
DISPOSABLE DIAPERS
DIET
diet
infant formula

CHEESECAKE...FUDGE RIPPLE... CHOCOLATE ECLAIRS...COOKIES...
ICE CREAM
FUDGE RIPPLE

I'M VERY ATTRACTED TO THIS MAN...BUT I'M TIRED. I JUST DON'T HAVE THE ENERGY TO PUT MY FEELINGS ON THE LINE FOR SOMEONE NEW.
WAIT HERE FOR NEXT AVAILABLE TELLER

I'M SO INTRIGUED BY HER... ..BUT I'VE MADE TOO MANY MISTAKES WITH WOMEN. I'M NOT ABOUT TO MAKE A MOVE UNLESS SHE LETS ON THAT SHE'S INTERESTED.

MAY I HELP YOU?

FIND OUT IF HE SHE LIKES ME!

HERE, SWEETIE. HAVE HALF OF MY SANDWICH.
I WISH YOU WOULDN'T DO THAT, MOM.

NOT ONLY DO I NOT WANT YOUR SANDWICH, BUT I CAN'T STAND TO SEE YOU DEGRADE YOURSELF BY ALWAYS GIVING YOUR FOOD AWAY.

YOU'RE A PERSON TOO, MOM! YOU DESERVE AN ENTIRE SANDWICH!!

HERE, SWEETIE. HAVE MY MILKSHAKE.
OKAY.

HI. I'M DANIEL. HOW DO YOU FEEL ABOUT THE WHOLE MEN/WOMEN THING?

ARE YOUR BELIEFS STRONGER THAN YOUR ACTIONS OR VICE VERSA? IF YOU HAD A DAUGHTER RIGHT NOW, WOULD YOU CONSIDER YOURSELF A GOOD ROLE MODEL?

WHICH AUTHORS HAVE BEST CAPTURED HOW YOU FEEL? ARE YOUR RELATIONSHIPS MORE COMPLICATED NOW AND IF SO, IS IT PARTLY BECAUSE IT'S HARDER TO SAY YOU NEED SOMEONE WITHOUT APPEARING TO BE A HYPOCRITE?

WHATEVER HAPPENED TO "HELLO, BEAUTIFUL. WHAT'S YOUR SIGN?"
Guisewite

YES, OF COURSE, MR. PINKLEY.
CATHY

NO PROBLEM. I'M SURE THE TIME YOU SPEND WILL ULTIMATELY BE A BENEFIT TO THE CORPORATE IMAGE.

CERTAINLY... AS THE HEAD OF THIS DIVISION, IT'S CRUCIAL FOR YOU TO STAY ON TOP OF NEW DEVELOPMENTS SUCH AS THIS. I UNDERSTAND.
Guisewite

MR. PINKLEY WILL BE A LITTLE LATE TODAY. HE'S HAVING HIS COLORS DONE.

WHAT DOES "CRAB BORDELAISE" MEAN?
IT'S FRENCH FOR CELLULITE.

MOM, IF YOU'RE UPSET ABOUT SOMETHING, WOULD YOU JUST SAY WHAT IT IS?!
WELL. AREN'T WE GROUCHY TODAY?

I'M NOT GROUCHY. I JUST WISH YOU'D OPEN UP AND SAY WHAT'S ON YOUR MIND FOR ONCE!!

WHAT'LL IT BE, LADIES?
THE CRAB AND THE CLAM.
Guisewite

I KNEW IT. I KNEW YOU WERE UPSET.
BOO HOO HOO

MOM... EVERY WOMAN IS QUESTIONING HER PRIORITIES TODAY. GO AHEAD... CRY! SCREAM! UNLEASH THOSE ANXIETIES!!
BOO HOO

I'M NOT HAVING AN IDENTITY CRISIS, CATHY. I WAS WATCHING A TELEPHONE COMMERCIAL.

...SO MUCH FOR DAUGHTERLY INTUITION.

HUM, HUM
SNAP SNAP
FLOORS

LET'S GET PHYSICAL! PHYSICAL! I WANT TO GET PHYSICAL!
SNAP SNAP!
TAP TAP!
FLOORS

LET ME HEAR YOUR BODY TALK...YOUR BODY TALK! I WANT TO GET ANIMAL! ANIMAL! LET'S GET...

IT'S GETTING MORE AND MORE DANGEROUS TO SING ALONG WITH THE WORDS.

YOU WHAT? YOU WON'T? YOU...WAIT!

OOH, YOU CAUGHT ME OFF GUARD WITH THAT ONE, IRVING. JUST WAIT UNTIL NEXT TIME.

THE VERY NEXT TIME YOU DISAPPOINT ME, YOU ARE GOING TO GET A SPEECH THE LIKES OF WHICH YOU'VE NEVER HEARD BEFORE! HA, HA! I AM READY!!

HI, CATHY. WHAT ARE YOU DOING TONIGHT?
PRAYING THAT THE MAN I LOVE IS OUT DOING SOMETHING HIDEOUS.

I'M READY TO GO TO LUNCH IF YOU ARE, CHARLENE.
RODUCT ESTING INC.
RECEPTIONIST

GREAT. DID YOU FINISH THE SANMARK PROJECT ?
RODUCT ESTING INC.
RECEPTIONIST

NO, BUT I GOT TO A GOOD STOPPING POINT.

I LOST MY TYPEWRITER.
Guisewite

OKAY, NOW... I WON'T BE GONE LONG... JUST DINNER AND A MOVIE.

I'M TURNING ON THE LIGHTS BECAUSE IT WILL BE DARK WHEN I GET BACK, BUT THERE'S NOTHING TO WORRY ABOUT.

I'LL BE HOME BEFORE YOU KNOW IT. GOODBYE ! GOODBYE !!

SOMETHING TELLS ME I'VE GONE TOO LONG BETWEEN DATES.
Guisewite

JAZZ.
AH, JAZZ. I LOVE JAZZ.

AND CLASSICAL MUSIC. I LOVE CLASSICAL MUSIC.
AH, THE CLASSICS. I LOVE TO PUT ON A SYMPHONY WITH DINNER.

AND OPERA. I LOVE OPERA.
OPERA. YES! OPERA! OPERA!

WHY DON'T YOU PUT ON AN ALBUM, CATHY ?
YOU WANT PETER, PAUL AND MARY OR THE BEATLES ?
Guisewite

MY FRIEND OLLIE WROTE TO THE GOVERNMENT FOR INFORMATION ON SMALL BUSINESS SUBSIDIES.

FLO ORDERED BROCHURES ON SETTING UP SMALL BUSINESSES AND FINANCING BUSINESSES. HELEN SENT IN FOR "SMALL BUSINESS STRATEGIES," "BUSINESS STATISTICS" AND "YOUR BUSINESS AND YOU".
STATISTICS FOR YOUR BUSINESS
YOUR BUSINESS

TOMORROW WE'RE GOING TO SIT DOWN AND START TURNING OUR DREAMS INTO REALITY!
GOOD FOR YOU, MOM!

WE HAVE TO. WE RAN OUT OF THINGS TO SEND AWAY FOR.
GUISEWITE

FLO, WE HAVE GATHERED HERE TO DISCUSS NEW BUSINESS OPPORTUNITIES... NOT TO LISTEN TO YOU GLOAT ABOUT YOUR GRANDDAUGHTER.

IF YOU WHIP OUT THAT PHOTO ALBUM ONE MORE TIME, I WILL HAVE NO CHOICE BUT TO DISMISS YOU FROM THIS AND ALL FURTHER SESSIONS... ALL IN FAVOR, SAY "AYE!"

OH, SHE'S ADORABLE ...OOH, LOOK AT THIS ONE
OOH... ISN'T THAT SWEET... AW...
MOVE OVER, OLLIE.
GUISEWITE

IF YOUR CATHY WERE MARRIED LIKE MY DAUGHTERS...
FLO, I HAPPEN TO BE VERY PROUD OF CATHY'S INDEPENDENCE.

WHEN AND IF SHE DECIDES TO MARRY AND HAVE A FAMILY, SHE WILL BE DOING SO ON A SOLID FOUNDATION OF CONFIDENCE AND SELF-RESPECT!

MOM, I COULDN'T HELP OVERHEARING WHAT YOU SAID. THAT WAS BEAUTIFUL!

WHERE ARE MY GRANDCHILDREN??
FLO, WAIT! COME BACK!
GUISEWITE

I'M HERE! I FLOODED THE LAUNDRY ROOM...I SHORTED-OUT MY HAIRDRYER...I DUMPED THE COFFEE POT IN MY BRIEFCASE...I RIPPED MY HEM...
GATE 72
GATE

...AND I HAD TO LEAVE MY CAR STRANDED ON THE FREEWAY, BUT I'M HERE! I OVERCAME EVERY CRISIS AND GOT HERE ON TIME!!

THERE ARE 38 PLANES AHEAD OF US ON THE RUNWAY. WE SHOULD BE TAKING OFF IN ABOUT 2½ HOURS.
2½ HOURS?? I CAN'T BELIEVE IT!

I HAD TIME TO BREAK FIFTEEN MORE THINGS.
Guisewite

I'M GOING TO TRANSFER MY SAVINGS TO A LONG-TERM, HIGH-INTEREST ACCOUNT AND THAT'S THAT!

...BUT WHAT IF I DECIDE TO BUY A HOUSE THIS YEAR? WHAT IF I HAVE TO ACT FAST ON A HOT STOCK TIP? WHAT IF I WANT TO TAKE A WORLD CRUISE??

YES! I MIGHT TAKE A WORLD CRUISE...GO INTO LAND DEVELOPMENT WITH ONE OF THE PASSENGERS... ..SHE'LL INTRODUCE ME TO..YAAA! I CAN'T HAVE MY MONEY LOCKED UP!!

WHAT DID YOU DO WITH YOUR $500, CATHY?
NOTHING. BY THE TIME IT WAS MY TURN, I NEEDED IT TO RE-DECORATE THE BABY'S ROOM.
Guisewite

I'D BETTER GO. THIS CALL IS COSTING YOU A FORTUNE, CATHY.
OH, DON'T WORRY ABOUT IT, MARY...

...I'VE OWED YOU A LETTER FOR SIX MONTHS!
YOU STILL OWE ME A LETTER.

WHAT DO YOU MEAN, I STILL OWE YOU A LETTER?? I JUST TALKED TO YOU LONG DISTANCE FOR TWO HOURS!!
PHONE CALLS DON'T CANCEL OUT LETTER DEBTS. ONLY LETTERS CANCEL LETTER DEBTS.

AFTER SIX MONTHS, PEOPLE START TO TURN ON YOU.
Guisewite

SOMETIMES I GET THE FEELING THAT I'M JUST WANDERING AROUND BETWEEN LADIES' ROOMS, ANDREA.

I GO TO WORK...I GO CHECK MY OUTFIT IN THE LADIES' ROOM..I GO TO A MEETING.. ..I GO CHECK MY HAIR IN THE LADIES' ROOM...

BEFORE, DURING AND AFTER EVERY EVENT OF MY LIFE, I MAKE THIS RITUALISTIC STOP IN THE LADIES' ROOM!
WELL, WHAT ARE YOU GOING TO DO TO CHANGE IT, CATHY?

I THINK MAYBE I'LL JUST STAY IN HERE.
SOAP
SOAP
Guisewite

I'M SORRY I MISSED THE PARTY LAST NIGHT, IRVING.
CATHY

I KNOW IT WAS IMPORTANT TO YOU, BUT I PROMISED MR. PINKLEY I'D WORK LATE.
CATHY, THOSE PEOPLE ARE ABUSING YOU.
CATHY

MR. PINKLEY CONTROLS YOUR WHOLE LIFE! AND YOU KNOW WHAT? HE'S GOING TO KEEP ON DOING IT IF YOU DON'T DEMAND A LIFE OF YOUR OWN.

I KNOW, HONEY...LOOK, I'LL MAKE IT UP TO YOU TONIGHT.
I CAN'T. I HAVE TO WORK LATE.
CATHY
Guisewite

"NOTICE TO ALL CUSTOMERS: ALL DRESSING ROOMS IN THIS STORE MAY BE MONITORED FOR SECURITY REASONS."

WHAT IS THE MEANING OF THIS SIGN??
OH, DON'T WORRY ABOUT IT.

THAT'S JUST UP THERE TO SCARE OFF SHOPLIFTERS.
THAT'S A RELIEF.

HERE...THIS WASN'T QUITE WHAT I WAS LOOKING FOR.
GOOD DECISION. I THOUGHT IT LOOKED RIDICULOUS ON YOU.
Guisewite

I TOLD JOAN HER BOYFRIEND WAS TAKING ADVANTAGE OF HER AND THAT SHE SHOULD DUMP HIM,

THEN JOAN TOLD ME MY BOYFRIEND WAS TAKING ADVANTAGE OF ME AND THAT I SHOULD DUMP HIM.

THEN WE SCREAMED AT EACH OTHER FOR NOT UNDERSTANDING AND WENT HOME TO OUR BOYFRIENDS.

WE'RE GETTING BETTER AT CONFRONTING EACH OTHER'S PROBLEMS.
Guisewite

IT'S MY PRIVILEGE TO PRESENT YOU WITH A RAISE TODAY, CATHY.
PINKLEY

YOU'RE DEVOTED, ENTHUSIASTIC, RESPONSIBLE, PRODUCTIVE AND INNOVATIVE.

WE ALL KNOW YOU DESERVE A RAISE... YET, I THINK YOU'LL FIND THIS SUM BEYOND YOUR WILDEST EXPECTATIONS...

2 MILLION DOLLARS!!
I FORGOT WHO I WAS DEALING WITH.
Guisewite

I GOT A RAISE, IRVING! I GOT A RAISE AND I DIDN'T EVEN HAVE TO BEG FOR IT!!

I AM FINALLY NEEDED, APPRECIATED, AND REWARDED! OH, IRVING, I WANT TO SAVOR THIS MOMENT FOREVER!!

I'M THRILLED FOR YOU, CATHY. I GOT LAID OFF TODAY.

I WAS HOPING FOREVER WOULD LAST LONGER THAN THAT.

YOU WERE LAID OFF? OH, IRVING, YOU MUST FEEL TERRIBLE. YOU MUST FEEL SO REJECTED AND USELESS.

YOU CAN LEAN ON ME, IRVING. GO AHEAD... CRY. JUST GET IT OUT OF YOUR SYSTEM... CRY! CRY!

WAAAH!
Guisewite

YOU'LL FIND ANOTHER JOB, IRVING. LOOK. THERE MUST BE 500 ADS IN THIS NEWSPAPER.
GREAT.

OH, IRVING... I KNOW IT'S HARD... BUT YOU'RE NOT ALONE. THERE ARE 9 MILLION PEOPLE OUT OF WORK RIGHT NOW!

THERE ARE 9 MILLION PEOPLE OUT OF WORK AND 500 ADS IN THE NEWSPAPER?

THANK YOU, CATHY. I FEEL MUCH BETTER NOW.
I HATE COMFORTING.
Guisewite

I GOT LAID OFF.

HOW COULD THIS HAPPEN TO ME? I'M YOUNG. I'M HANDSOME. I'M BRILLIANT. I'M CHARMING.

YAAAA!
CRASH

I GOT LAID OFF AND I JUST LOST MY SECURITY DEPOSIT.
Guisewite

I'M HAPPY TO FORMALLY ANNOUNCE CATHY'S PROMOTION TO THE LOWER RUNG OF MANAGEMENT AT PRODUCT TESTING, INC.
OH, NO. NOT TODAY. NO..NO!

CATHY'S UNWAVERING COMMITMENT TO WHAT SHE BELIEVES IN MAKES HER A LEADER WE CAN ALL TURN TO FOR FOCUS AND STRENGTH...
..CATHY, HOW ABOUT A FEW WORDS?

THE SALES CLERK MADE ME BUY IT.

IRVING GOT LAID OFF AND I GOT A PROMOTION. WHAT DO I SAY TO REASSURE HIM??
WHY DON'T YOU SEND HIM A NICE BALLOON-O-GRAM?

MY GENERATION HAPPENS TO BELIEVE IN TALKING, MOM. WE CONFRONT OUR FEELINGS.
DING DONG!

WHY COULDN'T YOU HAVE GOTTEN LAID OFF LAST MONTH, WHEN I HAD TIME TO COPE WITH IT??

WE CONFRONT OUR FEELINGS. THEN WE SEND A BALLOON-O-GRAM.

THEY'VE ALL SEEN MY PICTURE BY NOW, AND THEY'VE ALL READ ABOUT MY BIG PROMOTION.

THEY'RE PROBABLY ALL LOOKING AT ME... MAYBE THEY'RE EVEN A LITTLE INTIMIDATED.

OH, BUT THAT'S SO SILLY... I'M THE SAME PERSON I ALWAYS WAS. HA, HA! I'M APPROACHABLE... I'M GRACIOUS ...MY AUTOGRAPH? OH.. WELL, OF COURSE I'LL TAKE THE TIME...

IT'S HARD TO BE HUMBLE WHEN NOBODY READS THE COMPANY NEWSLETTER.
up
down

MOM, WHAT ARE YOU GOING TO DO WITH 900 COPIES OF THE COMPANY NEWSLETTER THAT HAS MY PICTURE IN IT?

I'M GOING TO TAKE THEM DOWN TO THE SHOPPING MALL, SET UP A LITTLE BOOTH OUTSIDE THE HOT PRETZEL STAND AND FORCE PERFECT STRANGERS TO READ ABOUT YOU!

OH... I'M SORRY, MOM. I DIDN'T MEAN TO INSULT YOU. YOU CAN HAVE AS MANY COPIES AS YOU WANT.

WHAT DID SHE THINK I WAS GOING TO DO WITH THEM?
HOT PRETZEL
Read about my daughter
GUISEWITE

WHAT'S ON TV TONIGHT, CATHY?
LET'S SEE... THERE'S A 92-YEAR-OLD MAN WHO TRAINED HIS COCKROACHES TO PLAY MOZART CONCERTOS...

... A WOMAN WHO CLAIMS SHE CAN EAT A 7-PIECE PATIO SET IN 45 MINUTES... A 3-YEAR OLD WHO BUILT A MICROWAVE OVEN OUT OF PLAYPEN PARTS...

... A COW IN MILWAUKEE THAT SAVED A FAMILY OF 12... AND A GRANDMOTHER WHO DOES A TRAMPOLINE ACT OVER A PIT OF WILD BOARS.

EH... SAME OLD STUFF.
GUISEWITE

HI! MAY I HELP YOU FIND SOMETHING FOR YOUR STUNNINGLY PETITE FIGURE?
I'M JUST LOOKING, THANKS.
SALAD SALAD

FINE. IF YOU NEED HELP, JUST ASK ME. I'M MARGARET. YOUR HAIR IS JUST LOVELY. WANT ME TO PUT THAT IN A DRESSING ROOM FOR YOU?
NO. I WAS JUST LOOKING AT IT.
NEW FOR

TAKE YOUR TIME. JUST REMEMBER ME. MARGARET. THAT COLOR WOULD BE BEAUTIFUL AGAINST YOUR FLAWLESS COMPLEXION.
MARGARET, I SWEAR I WON'T LET ANYONE ELSE WAIT ON ME!!

WHERE'S MARGARET?
SHE WENT OUT TO LUNCH.
DRESSING ROOMS
NO ONE ADMITTED WITHOUT A SALESPERSON.
GUISEWITE

YOU'RE TURNING INTO A VEGETABLE, IRVING. LOOK AT YOU.

YOU GOT LAID OFF AND YOU'RE JUST TURNING INTO A VEGETABLE.

YEAH? I SUPPOSE YOU'D HANDLE IT BETTER??

WELL, I CERTAINLY WOULDN'T TURN INTO A VEGETABLE!!

I'D TURN INTO A PEPPERIDGE FARM CAKE.

I DIDN'T FEEL LIKE SHAVING. SO WHAT?

IT'S NORMAL, IRVING. GROWING A BEARD IS A SYMBOLIC VALIDATION OF THE MASCULINITY THAT'S BEEN THREATENED BY THE LOSS OF YOUR JOB.

I CAN GET A NEW JOB ANY TIME I WANT.

YES. BUT HAVE YOU TRIED? NO. APPLYING FOR A JOB MEANS ADMITTING TO THE WORLD THAT YOU WERE NOT INDISPENSABLE BEFORE.

GET OUT OF HERE, CATHY!!

I UNDERSTAND. BY ATTACKING ME YOU ARE MERELY REDIRECTING THE ANGER YOU FEEL TOWARDS YOURSELF. HERE. LET ME HUG YOU.

PSYCHOLOGY IS A THANKLESS BUSINESS.

YOU HAVE COMPANY, IRVING? IS IT SOMEONE YOU USED TO WORK WITH?

NO. IT...UH, IT WORKS IN INVESTMENTS.

I SEE. HOW LONG WILL IT BE THERE?

WELL, IT JUST GOT HERE.

IS IT A RELATIVE?

NO. UH, YOU DON'T KNOW IT.

COULD I MEET IT?

UM...NO. I THINK SHE...

SHE! AHAH! AHAH!! I GOT YOU TO SAY "SHE"!

WHAT AM I CELEBRATING FOR?

WHATEVER HAPPENED TO WALLETS THAT MADE A HAPPY "SNAP!" SOUND WHEN YOU OPENED THEM?
PASSE. WE'RE INTO VELCRO NOW. IT RIPS OPEN.
WALLETS
RIP!

SEE? -RIP! - THE VELCRO "RIIIP!" IS THE LOOK AND THE SOUND OF THE 80'S SHOPPER.
IT SOUNDS LIKE THE WALLET IS SCREAMING EVERY TIME YOU OPEN IT.
RIIP!

PRECISELY. AND IT CAN BE YOURS FOR JUST $21.95.
YAAAA!
ALLETS
RIP!

I SEE YOUR POINT.
ETS

HO, HUM. I THINK YOU'D BETTER TAKE ME HOME, EDWARD.
OKAY, CATHY.

YOU'RE KIDDING. YOU'RE NOT GOING TO HASSLE ME ABOUT STAYING? NO BEGGING? NO SNEAK ATTACKS? NO "HOW ABOUT A QUICK BACK MASSAGE, HONEY?"?
DON'T BE SILLY. LET'S GO.

OH, EDWARD, I LOVE YOU FOR THIS!!!
HEH, HEH, HEH...
KISS
KISS
KISS

TAKE ME HOME, EDWARD.

HI, CATHY. ARE YOU IN THE MIDDLE OF ANYTHING?
IT'S APRIL 10, ANDREA. OF COURSE I'M IN THE MIDDLE OF SOMETHING.

WILL YOU BE BUSY ALL EVENING?
IT'S APRIL 10. OF COURSE I'LL BE BUSY ALL EVENING.

WHAT ARE YOU DOING?
ANDREA, IT'S APRIL 10. WHAT DO YOU THINK I'M DOING??!

Dear Aunt Dorothy, Thank you for the lovely scarf you sent for Christmas...

YOU'RE WORKING TOO HARD, CATHY. WHY DON'T YOU GO FRESHEN UP?

A LITTLE SPLASH OF WATER CAN BE AS REFRESHING AS A SHORT NAP.

ONCE AN OVER-ACHIEVER, ALWAYS AN OVER-ACHIEVER.
TOWE
Guiscwitz

I'VE BEEN SO BUSY...THANKS FOR HELPING WITH MY TAX RETURNS, IRVING.
NO PROBLEM. FOR EVERY NIGHT YOU'VE WORKED LATE, I SIMPLY ADDED $300 TO YOUR "AMOUNT DUE".
FORMS

I ADDED $450 FOR REFUSING TO DO MY LAUNDRY, AND $475 FOR REFUSING TO COOK MY DINNER.

I ADDED $1200 FOR THAT WEEKEND YOU SPENT IN ST. LOUIS WITH THAT TWERP ... AND 75¢ FOR EACH TIME IN 1981 THAT YOU SAID "I HATE FOOTBALL."

SO FAR, YOU OWE THE GOVERNMENT $26,000.00.
SINGLE PEOPLE ARE ALWAYS THE HARDEST HIT AT TAX TIME.

THANKS FOR COMING, CATHY. LIKE OUR AD SAYS, WE ARE THE COMPLETE TAX PREPARATION CENTER.
THE COMPLETE TAX PREP CENTER

WE EXAMINE YOUR TAX HISTORY... WE DIG FOR EVERY DEDUCTION... WE SCRUTINIZE EVERY CLAUSE... WE SEARCH OUT EACH AND EVERY LOOPHOLE!

SHOULDN'T THAT HAVE TAKEN MORE THAN THREE MINUTES?
Guiscwitz

I PAID MY INCOME TAXES.

IF I SELL ALL MY POSSESSIONS, QUIT USING ELECTRICITY AND GAS, CHOP MY FURNITURE UP FOR FIREWOOD...

... AND START SEWING MY OWN CLOTHES OUT OF OLD BEDSPREAD MATERIAL, I HAVE A CHANCE OF BREAKING EVEN THIS YEAR.

I'M STARTING TO SEE WHY THE "PRAIRIE LOOK" IS IN.

DID YOU SEE THIS, ANDREA? ...IF I LEAVE MY PANS AND COOKING UTENSILS LYING AROUND ON THE COUNTER, I LOOK LIKE A SLOB.

HOWEVER, IF I HANG THESE SAME PANS AND SPATULAS FROM THE CEILING AND WALLS, I INSTANTLY CREATE THE LOOK OF A GOURMET COOK!

PANS ON THE COUNTER: SLOB. PANS HANGING FROM THE CEILING: SOPHISTICATE. HA, HA! IT'S SO EASY!!

YOU'RE SUPPOSED TO WASH THEM FIRST, CATHY.
THERE'S ALWAYS A CATCH...

YOU ALWAYS SAID IT WOULDN'T MATTER WHICH ONE OF US WAS MAKING MORE MONEY, REMEMBER?

SO WHAT IF I GOT A PROMOTION? SO WHAT THAT YOU'RE LAID OFF?

IRVING, WE'RE TWO PEOPLE WHO LOVE EACH OTHER! WHAT DIFFERENCE DOES MONEY MAKE??!

THE LADY'S BUYING.
THAT'LL BE $78.00.
WAIT A MINUTE...

HI. I'M CALLING ABOUT THE TOP LEVEL MANAGEMENT POSITION YOU HAVE OPEN.
SORRY. THAT POSITION HAS BEEN FILLED BY A DONKEY-KONG GAME.
CLASSIFIEDS

WITH JUST A FEW VIDEO GAMES, WE FIGURE WE CAN BRING IN THE KIND OF BIG BUCKS THAT A WHOLE OFFICE FULL OF TOP MANAGEMENT COULDN'T PRODUCE.

IS THAT SO?! WELL, I'D LIKE TO HEAR THAT FROM THE PRESIDENT!!
CLASSIFIEDS

SORRY. HE'S UNDERGOING REPAIRS RIGHT NOW.
PRESIDENT
PAC-MAN
254
Guisewite

WHAT DO YOU MEAN, THE JOB IS FILLED? THE NEWSPAPER JUST CAME OUT FOURTEEN SECONDS AGO!
CIRCULATION

DO YOU HAVE ANY IDEA HOW MANY CALLS I'VE MADE? DO YOU HAVE ANY IDEA HOW MUCH I HATE BEGGING SOME TWERP TO GLANCE AT MY RESUME??

YOU WANT TO KNOW WHY I DON'T HAVE A JOB?? BECAUSE THE WORLD IS FULL OF YO-YO'S LIKE YOU!
LOOK ON THE BRIGHT SIDE, IRVING.

AT LEAST YOU DON'T WORK IN THE PERSONNEL DEPARTMENT.
Guisewite

I WAS REJECTED BY 47 MORE COMPANIES TODAY, CATHY. WANT TO HAVE DINNER?
UM... THAT ALL DEPENDS, IRVING.

WILL YOU ALWAYS LOVE ME FOR STANDING BY YOU IN YOUR TIME OF NEED.... OR WILL YOU RESENT ME FOR BEING THE ONE PERSON WHO SAW YOU DURING THIS MISERABLE PERIOD OF YOUR LIFE?

...I SEE. OH, IRVING, ISN'T THAT SWEET?

HE WANTS IT TO BE A SURPRISE.
Guisewite

♪ HI, IRVING! LOOK AT THIS GREAT JOB-HUNTING GUIDE I FOUND FOR YOU!! ♪ ♪ ♪ ♪

CATHY, DO YOU HAVE ANY IDEA HOW ANNOYING IT IS FOR A MAN TO HAVE HIS GIRLFRIEND CHEERFULLY LEAPING AROUND WHILE HE'S ON THE BRINK OF DISASTER?

MOTHERS CHEERFULLY LEAP AROUND. GIRLFRIENDS DO NOT CHEERFULLY LEAP AROUND.

WHAT DID I DO NOW?
FLOUR
SUGAR
Guisewite

I'M SO BUSY, I DON'T HAVE TIME TO EAT.
CATHY

I'M SO BUSY, I DON'T HAVE TIME TO EAT A DONUT.

I'M SO BUSY, I DON'T HAVE TIME TO EAT A DONUT COVERED WITH GOOEY CHOCOLATE FROSTING.
COFFEE RULES
donuts

I'M TOO BUSY TO BE ON A DIET.
CATHY
Guisewite

IF I WEAR THE OUTFIT I LOOK BEST IN ON MY FIRST DATE WITH THIS MAN, I WON'T HAVE ANYTHING TO WEAR IF I EVER GO OUT WITH HIM AGAIN.

THEN AGAIN, IF I DON'T WEAR WHAT I LOOK BEST IN, I'LL BE UNCOMFORTABLE ALL NIGHT, I'LL ACT WEIRD, AND THERE WON'T BE A SECOND DATE.

THEN AGAIN, IF I WEAR THE GREAT OUTFIT AND WE HAVE A WONDERFUL TIME, I'LL HAVE TO BUY A WHOLE NEW WARDROBE TO LIVE UP TO THE FIRST IMPRESSION I MADE.

I DECIDED TO STAY HOME AND WATCH TV.
Guisewite

HI, IRVING. WOULD YOU MIND PICKING UP MY DRY CLEANING TODAY?
CATHY

CATHY, JUST BECAUSE I'M NOT GOING INTO A REGULAR OFFICE DOESN'T MEAN I HAVE NOTHING TO DO.
CATHY

I HAVE INTERVIEWS TO SET UP... CALLS TO MAKE... RESUMES TO PREPARE... I DO NOT HAVE TIME TO RUN AROUND DOING YOUR ERRANDS!

PEOPLE WHO WORK AT HOME GET NO RESPECT.
CLICK!
PLAYBOY
Guisewitz

I'D LIKE A BREATH MINT, BUT I DON'T WANT TO BE SO OBVIOUS ABOUT PREPARING FOR A BIG KISS AT THE DOOR.

I COULD OFFER HIM A BREATH MINT, BUT THEN I'D BE REALLY OBVIOUS... I COULD TRY TO SECRETLY EAT A BREATH MINT, BUT THAT WOULD BE REALLY, REALLY OBVIOUS... I..
BYE, CATHY. SEE YOU SOON.

THE STORY OF MY LIFE. A MOUTHFUL OF BREATH MINTS, AND NO ONE TO KISS.
Guisewitz

EVERYWHERE YOU GO, THERE'S TOO MUCH STUFF TO BUY. I WENT TO THE DRUGSTORE FOR A TUBE OF TOOTHPASTE, I CAME OUT WITH A DINETTE SET.

I WENT TO THE GAS STATION FOR GAS, I CAME HOME WITH A 5-PIECE LUGGAGE ENSEMBLE.

I WENT TO THE CARD SHOP FOR A CARD, I CAME AWAY WITH AN ESPRESSO MACHINE. YOUR FATHER IS JUST GOING TO KILL ME.
WHERE IS DAD?

HE RAN OUT FOR A NEWSPAPER.
Guisewitz

OOH, IRVING, LET'S GO HEAR JAMES LEE STANLEY PLAY.
FORGET IT, CATHY. I KNOW HOW WOMEN ARE.

THE GUY SINGS A FEW SONGS... YOU GAZE AT HIS FACE... YOU GET CAUGHT UP IN HIS LYRICS... AND BY THE END OF ONE SET, YOU'RE LOOKING AT ME LIKE I HAVE CROSSED EYES.

I AM SICK OF PAYING TEN BUCKS SO MY DATE CAN FALL IN LOVE WITH SOME MUSICIAN!!
FINE. WHAT DO YOU WANT TO DO TONIGHT?

LET'S SEE IF OLIVIA NEWTON-JOHN IS IN TOWN.
GUISEWITE

WHERE HAVE YOU BEEN ALL EVENING, CATHY??
I WENT TO HEAR JAMES LEE STANLEY. YOU DIDN'T WANT TO GO IRVING, REMEMBER?

IT WAS GREAT, IRVING. MY SEAT WAS PERFECT... THE SONGS WERE WONDERFUL... THE MUSIC WAS TREMENDOUS...

THE AUDIENCE WAS SCREAMING FOR ENCORES... IT WAS ONE OF THE FINEST EVENINGS OF MY LIFE!!

DID YOU MISS ME, HONEY?
GUISEWITE

THE HOT NEW LOOK FOR SPRING IS THE LONG, FLOWERY, RUFFLED PRAIRIE LOOK.

THE HOT NEW LOOK IS ALSO FLASHY STRIPES WITH FAT PUNK BELTS... AND THE HOT NEW LOOK IS PASTEL MILITARY MINI-SKIRTS. THEY ARE ALL THE HOT NEW LOOK.

THESE ARE TOTALLY DIFFERENT THINGS. THEY CAN'T ALL BE THE HOT NEW LOOK.
THEY ARE ALL EQUALLY THE HOT NEW LOOK!

IT LOOKS LIKE ANOTHER GOOD YEAR TO BUY SHOES.
WAIT UP.
GUISEWITE

DID YOU HAVE A NICE WEEKEND, CATHY?
YES, MR. PINKLEY. I WENT TO THE SYMPHONY WITH A MAN I JUST MET.

HE OPENED MY EYES TO A WHOLE NEW WORLD AND MADE ME REALIZE HOW TRIVIAL AND MEANINGLESS MY BUSINESS PROBLEMS ARE.

THIS IS STUPID, BORING, DISGUSTING WORK, MR. PINKLEY. MY JOB MAKES ME SICK!!

...NEVER REPORT ON YOUR WEEKEND BEFORE YOU'VE HAD YOUR COFFEE.
CATHY

I CANNOT BELIEVE YOU SPENT MORE MONEY ON CLOTHES, CATHY.
ACCESSORIES, IRVING.

ACCESSORIES ARE THE KEY FOR THE SMART 80's SHOPPER.
WHAT DID YOU GET TALKED INTO NOW?

..WITH JUST ONE VERSATILE SCARF, I CAN SOLVE ALL MY WARDROBE PROBLEMS!!
HAH!

HM! IT WORKS BETTER THAN I THOUGHT.

I AM TOTALLY ATTRACTED TO THIS MAN, AND I WANT HIM TO KNOW IT.
MENU

IT'S TIME WOMEN LEARNED TO TAKE THE INITIATIVE AND TAKE A CHANCE!

THERE! I'VE DONE IT! MY FEELINGS ARE KNOWN AND IT'S UP TO HIM TO REACT!!

WHAT DID YOU SAY TO LET THIS MAN KNOW YOU WERE SO INTERESTED, CATHY?
MY ELBOW TOUCHED HIS ARM.

MY BLUE SKIRT AND MY TAN JACKET ARE GETTING DRY CLEANED.

MY GREEN DRESS IS HAVING A NEW ZIPPER PUT IN. MY LAVENDER BLOUSE IS WAITING FOR BUTTONS.

MY WHITE SLACKS AND ALL MY UNDERWEAR ARE IN THE WASHING MACHINE.

I WON'T BE IN TODAY, MR. PINKLEY. MY CLOTHES ARE ALL BUSY.
Guisewite

I KNOW UNEMPLOYMENT IS HARD ON YOU, IRVING, BUT I DON'T WANT IT TO DRIVE US APART.

YOUR TRIUMPHS ARE **OUR** TRIUMPHS... YOUR DISASTERS ARE **OUR** DISASTERS...

IRVING, IF WE CAN JUST LEARN TO SHARE, NOTHING WILL EVER COME BETWEEN US!!
RING RING

...IT'S OUR OTHER GIRLFRIEND.
Guisewite

14 RINGS... 15 RINGS... COME ON, IRVING, ANSWER YOUR PHONE.
RING! RING!

19... 20... 21... I KNOW YOU'RE THERE, IRVING, AND I'M GOING TO LET IT RING UNTIL I TALK TO YOU!
RING! RING!

CATHY, EXACTLY HOW GOOD OF A CONVERSATION DO YOU EXPECT TO HAVE WITH A MAN WHO'S LET HIS PHONE RING 26 TIMES BEFORE ANSWERING IT??
RING RING RING
....HELLO?
GLFKT.

YOU MADE ME NERVOUS.
Guisewite

NO, I WILL NOT STAY LATE AGAIN, MR. PINKLEY. MY PERSONAL RELATIONSHIPS ARE UNDER A BIG ENOUGH STRAIN WITHOUT ADDING ANOTHER MIDNIGHT AT THE OFFICE.

IF YOU CONTINUE TO MAKE THESE OUTRAGEOUS DEMANDS, YOU'RE GOING TO HAVE TO JUST FIND YOURSELF ANOTHER SLAVE!
PINKLEY

IT'S HARD TO BELIEVE I PUT MY CAREER ON THE LINE FOR A "THREE'S COMPANY" RERUN.
Guisewite

WELL, UM, MAYBE WE CAN GET TOGETHER SOMETIME, CATHY... MAYBE I'LL GIVE YOU A CALL NEXT WEEK... MAYBE WE'LL GET SOME DINNER... WELL, MAYBE. WE'LL SEE...

MEN ARE LUNATICS, ANDREA.
YOU JUST EXPECT TOO MUCH, CATHY.

WHEN ARE YOU GOING TO REALIZE THERE'S NO SUCH THING AS "MR. RIGHT"?
ANDREA, I **KNOW** THERE'S NO SUCH THING AS MR. RIGHT.

...THEY'RE ALL MR. MAYBE'S.
Guisewite

I'M WEARING "THE PROVOCATIVE NEW COLOGNE FOR WOMEN." HE'S WEARING "THE DARING NEW MEN'S COLOGNE."

THE ROOM IS CHARGED WITH ELECTRICITY.

I THINK OUR COLOGNES ARE HAVING A PARTY IN MID-AIR.
Guisewite

I JUST WANT TO KNOW IF HE'S GOING TO CALL, ANDREA... IF HE CALLS, IT'S FINE. IF HE DOESN'T CALL, IT'S FINE.

I JUST WANT TO KNOW IF HE'S GOING TO CALL SO I CAN QUIT WONDERING ABOUT IT.

RING RING!
HE'S CALLING! HE'S CALLING!

THANK HEAVENS. ARE YOU FINALLY SATISFIED NOW?
...I JUST WANT TO KNOW IF HE'S GOING TO CALL AGAIN...
Guisewite

IT USED TO BE A BAD DAY IF MY HAIR DIDN'T TURN OUT.
IN

THEN IT WAS A BAD DAY IF I SPILLED COFFEE IN MY FILE DRAWER 10 MINUTES BEFORE A CLIENT CAME IN.

NOW IT ISN'T A BAD DAY UNLESS I LOSE MY BRIEF-CASE, HAVE 20 PEOPLE YELLING AT ME SIMULTANEOUSLY, GET SENT OUT OF TOWN ON 3 MINUTES' NOTICE, AND ACCIDENTLY COLLATE MY RESUME IN WITH THE ANNUAL REPORT.

I'VE SET HIGHER STANDARDS FOR MYSELF.
Guisewite

DEAR MARY,
I HAVE MET A CHARMING NEW MAN WHO I PLAN TO SPEND A GREAT DEAL OF TIME WITH.

MY PROBLEMS WITH IRVING ARE IN THE PAST! HE HAS NO PLACE IN THE DYNAMIC NEW DIRECTION MY LIFE IS TAKING...
DING DONG!

IRVING!
CATHY, I HAVE TO MOVE IN WITH YOU FOR A FEW DAYS. I'M DESPERATE!!

I HATE IT WHEN A SITUATION DETERIORATES BEFORE I FINISH THE LETTER.
RIP!
Guisewite

MOVE IN WITH ME? ARE YOU CRAZY, IRVING?? WE'RE HARDLY SPEAKING!
I KNOW YOU HATE ME FOR ASKING, CATHY, BUT I'VE BEEN OUT OF WORK FOR 8 WEEKS.

I CAN'T FIND A JOB, I CAN'T PAY MY BILLS, I'VE LOST MY APARTMENT, AND I HAVE NO WHERE TO GO.

I KNOW I'M BEING A HIDEOUS BURDEN JUST WHEN YOU MOST LOVE YOUR INDEPENDENCE... BUT PLEASE, LET ME SLEEP ON YOUR FLOOR FOR A FEW NIGHTS AND I'LL GET OUT OF YOUR LIFE FOREVER.

UNDERSTANDING IS A VICIOUS WEAPON.
Guisewite

MOM, REMEMBER WHAT YOU SAID WHEN I TOLD YOU SUE WAS LIVING WITH RICHARD?
YES. I SAID, "WELL, THERE GOES ANOTHER MODERN YOUNG COUPLE".

WHAT DID YOU SAY WHEN I TOLD YOU MARK WAS MOVING IN WITH KAREN?
I SAID, "WELL, THERE GOES ANOTHER MODERN YOUNG COUPLE".

WELL, IRVING AND...
YAAAA!!

JUST CHECKING.
Guisewite

YOU MAY STAY HERE, IRVING, BUT YOU MAY NOT MOVE YOUR STUFF IN HERE!
BUT CATHY, I LOST MY APARTMENT ... WHERE CAN I PUT IT?

FORGET IT, IRVING.
OH, PLEASE, PLEASE...
MY APARTMENT IS TOO SMALL.
PLEASE. IT WON'T TAKE MUCH ROOM.
IT IS OUT OF THE QUESTION!!
BUT CATHY...

HI, CATHY. I'M HERE WITH ALL MY STUFF.

I WAS TIRED OF FIGHTING ABOUT IT.
Guisewite

YOU HEARD ME, IRVING. I WANT LIVER FOR DINNER.
EVERY TIME YOU FEEL GUILTY ABOUT SOMETHING, YOU START WORRYING ABOUT YOUR NUTRITION.

YOU FIGURE YOU'LL FEEL BETTER ABOUT HAVING ME SECRETLY STAYING HERE IF YOU EAT A DINNER YOUR MOTHER WOULD APPROVE OF.

YOU'RE NUTS, CATHY! NOBODY IN THE WORLD IS AS NUTS AS YOU ARE!!

AT LEAST I KNOW SHE'S EATING RIGHT.
GUISEWITE

HOW DID YOU FIND OUT THAT IRVING IS STAYING AT MY APARTMENT, MOM?
FLO TOLD ME.

FLO TOLD ME. FLO TOLD HER NEIGHBORS. HER NEIGHBORS TOLD THEIR CO-WORKERS.

THEIR CO-WORKERS ALERTED ALL THEIR RELATIVES, WHO SET UP A COAST-TO-COAST HOTLINE...AND FOR THOSE WHO MISSED OUT, STAY TUNED FOR THE 6:00 NEWS!

...THAT'S THE LAST TIME I ASK FLO TO SNEAK OVER TO YOUR PLACE AND FIND OUT WHAT'S GOING ON.
GUISEWITE

IRVING, YOUR DIRTY DISHES ARE IN MY SINK!
SO WHAT, CATHY? SO ARE YOURS!!

I DON'T WANT YOUR DIRTY DISHES TOUCHING MY DIRTY DISHES!!

YEAH? WELL, I DON'T WANT YOUR GARBAGE TOUCHING MY GARBAGE!!
THAT'S MY PAPER TOWEL! DON'T TOUCH MY PAPER TOWEL!!

IF MOTHERS ONLY KNEW HOW LITTLE THEY HAD TO WORRY ABOUT...
GUISEWITE

I LOVE YOU FOR LETTING ME STAY HERE WHILE I FIND A JOB, CATHY!
OH, IRVING...EVERYTHING WILL BE FINE. YOU'LL SEE!

BUT I HATE IT! I HATE DEPENDING ON A WOMAN LIKE THIS!!
AND I HATE HAVING YOU HERE! LOOK AT THIS MESS!!

BUT I DON'T KNOW WHAT ELSE TO DO! MY LIFE IS A WRECK!!
I KNOW, IRVING... WAAAH!!

WOMEN ARE SO MOODY.

CATHY ALWAYS MAKES GOOD DECISIONS FOR HERSELF!
WE CAN ALWAYS TRUST HER TO DO THE RIGHT THING!

SHE HAS EXCELLENT JUDGMENT!
SHE HAS SUCH A LEVEL HEAD ON HER SHOULDERS!

WE'RE SO LUCKY TO HAVE A DAUGHTER WITH HER BRAINS AND GOOD SENSE!
SHE'S WONDERFUL! PERFECT AND WONDERFUL!!

YOUR FATHER MOTHER IS WORRIED SICK!!

IT'S 6:30, CATHY. LET'S GO FRESHEN UP.
CHARLENE, WOMEN WHO FRESHEN UP BEFORE THEY GO HOME JUST PERPETUATE THE MYTH OF THE SUPER-WOMAN.

WHEN I GO HOME I WANT TO LOOK EXHAUSTED AND PATHETIC. EXHAUSTED, PATHETIC, WRINKLED, HAGGARD AND IN NEED OF A NICE HOT DINNER.

IRVING, I...
I HAD HIDEOUS INTERVIEWS ALL DAY AND I'M READY TO DROP. WILL YOU FIX ME A NICE HOT DINNER?

I CAN'T BELIEVE IT. I DON'T LOOK BAD ENOUGH.

PLEASE LET ME STAY ANOTHER DAY, CATHY. YOU'RE THE ONLY ONE I CAN TURN TO.
OH, NO. I'M NOT FALLING FOR THAT OLD LINE AGAIN.

PLEASE LET ME STAY, CATHY. I WILL NEVER TAKE OUR FRIENDSHIP FOR GRANTED AGAIN.
OH, NO. I'M NOT FALLING FOR THAT OLD LINE AGAIN.

PLEASE LET ME STAY, CATHY. BY HELPING ME, YOU'RE DOING YOUR PART TOWARDS RESTORING ORDER TO THESE TIMES OF ECONOMICAL AND EMOTIONAL CHAOS.
OKAY.

I HADN'T HEARD THAT ONE YET.
Guisewite

MY NEW BOYFRIEND ISN'T SPEAKING TO ME, MY MOM ISN'T SPEAKING TO ME, MY EX-BOYFRIEND IS ASLEEP ON MY COUCH AND I JUST GAINED 8 POUNDS.
OH, CATHY...

THEN AGAIN, MAYBE IT'S NOT SO BAD... SOMETIMES YOU HAVE TO FEEL TERRIBLE BEFORE YOU CAN BE MOTIVATED TO CHANGE SOMETHING.

SOMETIMES YOU CAN ONLY TURN YOUR LIFE AROUND AFTER YOU'VE REALLY HIT THE BOTTOM!
IN WHAT WAY IS A QUART OF ICE CREAM GOING TO HELP?
ICE CREAM

I'M NOT QUITE LOW ENOUGH.
ICE CREAM
Guisewite

AREN'T YOU NERVOUS ABOUT IRVING SNOOPING AROUND ALL YOUR STUFF WHILE YOU'RE AT WORK ALL DAY, CATHY?

ANDREA, IRVING AND I HAVE ALWAYS BEEN TOTALLY OPEN ABOUT OUR OTHER FRIENDSHIPS.

I HAVE NOTHING TO HIDE!!
GOOD FOR YOU! AND WHY DON'T YOU HAVE ANYTHING TO HIDE?!

I ALREADY HID EVERYTHING.
APTS.
Guisewite

YOU'RE WRINKLING UP MY COUCH... YOUR JUNK IS ALL OVER MY APARTMENT... BUT EATING MY DONUTS WAS THE FINAL STRAW!!
Z Z Z Z Z

WHAT DONUTS?
THERE WERE FOUR DONUTS IN THIS BOX, IRVING! WHERE ARE THEY?!

NEVER POINT THE GUILTY FINGER UNLESS YOU'RE SURE IT DOESN'T HAVE JELLY ON IT.
Guisewite

YOU'RE JUST HAVING AN OFF-DAY, CATHY.
IRVING, THE TIME YOU'VE SPENT HERE HAS BEEN AMONG THE WORST IN MY LIFE.

MAYBE YOU'RE HAVING AN OFF-WEEK.
I WANT MY APARTMENT TO MYSELF AGAIN. I WANT PEACE, QUIET AND NO MORE COMPANY!!

HI, IT'S DAVID. REMEMBER ME?

I'M HAVING AN OFF-LIFE.
Guisewite

ARE YOU ACTUALLY GOING TO LET THAT TWERP THAT YOU HAVEN'T HEARD FROM IN 6 MONTHS STAY HERE??
IRVING, DAVID MISSED A PLANE AND ALL THE HOTELS ARE FULL.

I DON'T SEE WHY THE TWO OF YOU CAN'T SHARE THE LIVING ROOM FLOOR.
CATHY, HE'S IMPOSING ON YOU!

IRVING, YOU'RE BOTH IMPOSING ON ME.

I WAS IMPOSING ON YOU FIRST!!
Guisewite

IRVING, YOU AND I BOTH NEEDED A PLACE TO STAY, AND WE BOTH PICKED CATHY'S LIVING ROOM.

I THINK WE SHOULD TALK ABOUT THIS. LET'S GET OUR FEELINGS OUT IN THE OPEN!

IT IS EXACTLY THESE AWKWARD MOMENTS THAT CAN BRING US CLOSER TO THE REAL TRUTHS IN HUMAN RELATIONSHIPS!!

NEVER BUY TWO MEN YOU'RE DATING THE SAME SWEATER FOR CHRISTMAS.

I'M IRVING. WHO ARE YOU?
PHILLIP. I USED TO GO OUT WITH CATHY. MIND IF I HAVE A SEAT UNTIL SHE GETS HOME FROM WORK?

I'M DAVID. WHO ARE YOU?
EMERSON. I USED TO GO OUT WITH CATHY. MIND IF I HAVE A SEAT UNTIL SHE GETS HOME FROM WORK?

WHO ARE YOU?
MARK. I USED TO GO OUT WITH CATHY. MIND IF I HAVE A SEAT UNTIL SHE GETS HOME FROM WORK?

WHEW! AFTER A DAY LIKE TODAY, THINGS CAN ONLY GET BETTER.

EVERY PERSON I'VE EVER DATED IN MY LIFE IS STANDING IN MY LIVING ROOM, ANDREA.
OH, CATHY...

WHY DOES THIS ALWAYS HAPPEN?? EITHER THERE'S NO ONE, OR ELSE EVERYONE IN THE WORLD SHOWS UP AT THE SAME TIME!
CATHY, THIS IS HORRIBLE! YOU HAVE TO DO SOMETHING!

REFRESHMENTS! I'LL GO TO THE STORE AND BUY SOME REFRESHMENTS!!

SUPERMARKET
SALE
SALE
donuts
pie

I TYPED UP THE NOTES FROM THE MEETING YOU MISSED THIS MORNING, CATHY.
THANKS, CHARLENE. I APPRECIATE IT.
CATHY

5 PEOPLE THINK YOU SHOULD THROW IRVING OUT... 3 PEOPLE THINK YOU SHOULD THROW DAVID OUT...

AND 14 PEOPLE WANT TO COME OVER AND WATCH THEM FIGHT.
I CAN'T BELIEVE THIS! GET BACK IN HERE, CHARLENE!!

WHICH WAY DID YOU VOTE?
Guisewite

DAVID AND IRVING, THIS IS NOT WORKING OUT! I CAN'T POSSIBLY TELL HOW I FEEL ABOUT EITHER OF YOU WHEN BOTH OF YOU ARE HERE!!

AHEM... I ALSO CAN'T TELL HOW I FEEL ABOUT EITHER OF YOU WHEN ONLY ONE OF YOU IS HERE.

I ALSO CAN'T TELL HOW I FEEL ABOUT EITHER OF YOU WHEN BOTH OF YOU ARE GONE. THEREFORE, I AM GOING TO GO WATCH TELEVISION.

NEVER DELIVER A SPEECH WHEN ALL YOU HAVE WRITTEN IS THE FIRST SENTENCE.
Guisewite

MY OFFICE CALLED, IRVING. I HAVE TO GET BACK TO ST. LOUIS.
.... WAIT A MINUTE. IF YOU LEAVE, CATHY WILL START MISSING YOU.

WOMEN ALWAYS MISS THE GUY WHO LEAVES FIRST. THIS IS A TRAP!
I HAVE TO LEAVE, IRVING. I HAVE A PLANE.

HAH! I WILL LEAVE FIRST!
THEN WE'RE BOTH LEAVING.
I AM LEAVING FIRST!

GOOD WORK, CATHY. I DIDN'T THINK YOU HAD THE HEART TO TELL THEM BOTH TO GO.
Guisewite

DAVID WENT BACK TO ST. LOUIS AND IRVING MOVED IN WITH HIS PARENTS. AT LEAST MY MOTHER WILL BE THRILLED.

IT WAS HORRIBLE TO SEE THEM LEAVE...BUT I JUST KEPT THINKING, "MOM IS GOING TO BE THRILLED".

SOME THINGS ARE WORTH GOING THROUGH IF ONLY BECAUSE YOU KNOW YOUR MOTHER WILL BE TOTALLY THRILLED!

...WHATEVER MAKES YOU HAPPY, DEAR.
GUISEWITE

RELATIONSHIPS ARE LIKE A GIANT PLATE OF SPAGHETTI, ANDREA.

EACH PIECE IS PERFECT BY ITSELF... BUT WHEN YOU PUT IT ALL TOGETHER, IT BECOMES A TANGLED MESS, IMPOSSIBLE TO SORT OUT.
VERY INTERESTING, CATHY.

USING THAT SAME THEORY, WE SEE THAT RELATIONSHIPS ARE ALSO LIKE A TINY TOSSED SALAD... AFTER BEING PART OF THE WHOLE, NO ONE PIECE IS EVER EXACTLY THE SAME.

DON'T BE RIDICULOUS.
GUISEWITE

"AMAZING NEW DIET BREAKTHROUGH! LOSE 15 POUNDS IN 7 DAYS!"

HA! WHAT TRASH!!

GOOD FOR YOU, CATHY. YOU'RE FINALLY GETTING MORE REALISTIC ABOUT YOUR WEIGHT-LOSS PROGRAMS!

I NEED TO FIND ONE WHERE I CAN LOSE 15 POUNDS IN 3 DAYS.
GUISEWITE

WITH OUR NEW VIDEO TAPE RECORDER, WE WATCHED THE 6:00 NEWS AT 8:45. WE SAW YESTERDAY'S 3:00 MOVIE AT 5:20 TODAY.
VTR

WE SAW TUESDAY'S 8:00 SPECIAL AT 9:00 SATURDAY MORNING, AND THE 7:30 SUNDAY SYMPHONY DURING LUNCH ON WEDNESDAY.
VTR

MOM, THAT'S GREAT TO BE ABLE TO WATCH SHOWS WHEN YOU WANT! WHAT ARE YOU AND DAD GOING TO DO WITH ALL YOUR NEW SPARE TIME?
VTR

WE'RE GOING TO TRY TO FIGURE OUT WHAT DAY IT IS.
Guisewitz

YOU'RE EATING INSTEAD OF FACING YOUR PROBLEMS AGAIN, CATHY.
WRONG, ANDREA.

EATING HAS A CALMING EFFECT THAT OFTEN ACTUALLY HELPS YOU FOCUS ON YOUR PROBLEMS MORE CLEARLY.

WHEN YOUR MOUTH IS BUSY EATING, IT FREES UP YOUR MIND SO YOU CAN THINK MORE LOGICALLY.
WHAT ARE YOU THINKING ABOUT?

I'M THINKING ABOUT WHAT I CAN EAT NEXT.
Guisewitz

I'VE CALLED THIS MEETING TO DISCUSS SOME NEW CONCEPTS IN MANAGEMENT FOR YOUR DEPARTMENTS.

ACCORDING TO THIS STUDY, IF YOUR EMPLOYEES ARE FRUSTRATED, DEPRESSED OR ABSORBED IN PERSONAL PROBLEMS, IT WILL ONLY NEGATIVELY AFFECT OUR CORPORATE GOAL.

IT IS SOMETIMES FAR MORE PRODUCTIVE FOR THESE EMPLOYEES TO ACTUALLY LEAVE THE OFFICE FOR A FEW...

I WASN'T FINISHED YET!!
Guisewitz

I WORRY. I THOUGHT, "CATHY MUST BE TOO SICK TO GET TO A PHONE!"
ONLY MY MOTHER COULD MAKE ME FEEL THIS GUILTY.
IN
IN
CATHY

IS YOUR JOB SO IMPORTANT THAT YOU CAN'T EVEN RETURN MY CALLS ANYMORE?!
ONLY A BOYFRIEND COULD MAKE ME FEEL THIS GUILTY.
IN
IN
CATHY

HOW DO YOU HAVE TIME FOR 14 BOYFRIENDS AND NOT HAVE 3 SECONDS TO CALL ME ??!
ONLY A GIRLFRIEND COULD MAKE ME FEEL THIS GUILTY.
IN
IN
CATHY

BAD NEWS, MOM. YOUR COMPETITION'S GETTING TOUGH.
IN
IN
CATHY
GUISEWITE

WHAT DO YOU THINK, CATHY? CAN YOU TURN YOUR JOB INTO SOMETHING MORE, OR WILL YOU CHANGE CAREERS?
SHAMPOO

WHERE DO YOU SEE YOURSELF 10 YEARS FROM NOW?
SHAMPOO

WHAT DO YOU THINK ABOUT CHILDREN? REAL ESTATE? RETIREMENT PLANNING?
SHAMPOO

I HAVEN'T EVEN FIGURED OUT IF MY HAIR IS "DRY", "NORMAL", OR "OILY" YET.
SHA
GUISEWITE

HOW DO YOU KNOW IRVING'S GOING TO PICK A FIGHT?
SIMPLE. HE'S WEARING HIS BLUE-STRIPED SHIRT TODAY.

EVERY TIME IRVING WANTS TO FIGHT HE WEARS HIS BLUE-STRIPED SHIRT. WHEN HE'S GUILTY, HE WEARS HIS YELLOW SWEATER. HE MAKES UP IN TAN, HE BREAKS UP IN GREEN. HE SULKS IN HIS BURGUNDY SWEATSUIT.

MEN ARE SO PREDICTABLE! THEY'RE ABSOLUTELY, TOTALLY, 100% PREDICTABLE!!
WHAT ARE YOU CHANGING FOR?

I WANT TO SLIP INTO MY HOLIER-THAN-THOU OUTFIT.
GUISEWITE

BOING!

SHOES
CRASH!

SPLAT!
GZKKK...
COFFEE
CAN OPENER
Groisewitz

I WON'T BE IN TODAY, MR. PINKLEY. I DON'T THINK I SHOULD BE ALLOWED NEAR A CAR.

I THOUGHT YOU INVITED ME OVER TO SCREAM AT ME, CATHY.
I DID, IRVING.

... BUT LISTEN TO THAT SONG ON THE RADIO. REMEMBER HOW HAPPY WE WERE WHEN THAT SONG FIRST CAME OUT?

YOU'RE NOT GOING TO SCREAM AT ME?
NOW THEY'RE PLAYING OUR OTHER FAVORITE SONG! OH, IRVING! IRVING!!

KISS
KISS
KISS
KISS
Groisewitz

WHERE'S THE REST OF THE COFFEE, MOM?
I DON'T KNOW. I MADE 3 CUPS.

MOM, "3 CUPS" ON THAT COFFEE MAKER DOESN'T EVEN FILL ONE MUG.
AT MY HOUSE "3 CUPS" MAKES 3 CUPS.

AT YOUR HOUSE YOU USE PUNY CUPS. IF YOU WANT TO MAKE 3 CONTEMPORARY MUGS OF COFFEE, YOU HAVE TO MAKE 7 CUPS!
7 CUPS! WE'LL NEVER FINISH 7 CUPS!!

HOW'S YOUR MOM?
I DON'T KNOW. BY THE TIME WE SAT DOWN TO TALK, WE WEREN'T SPEAKING TO EACH OTHER.
Groisewitz

HI, CATHY. IT'S DAVID.
HI. AHEM...

IT WAS GREAT SEEING YOU LAST WEEK.
AHEM... AHEM...

IS IRVING SITTING RIGHT THERE AND YOU CAN'T TALK?
YES! YES! THAT IS CORRECT! YES!!

SO. HOW'S DAVID?
WHAT MAKES YOU THINK THAT WAS DAVID ON THE PHONE?
Guisewite

OKAY. HERE COMES THE COMMERCIAL BREAK. I HAVE EXACTLY 3 MINUTES TO SAY SOMETHING CLEVER TO MY DATE.

I NOW HAVE 2½ MINUTES TO SAY SOMETHING THAT WILL LINGER IN THIS MAN'S MIND AND MAKE HIM DESPERATE TO GO OUT WITH ME AGAIN.

I NOW HAVE 45 SECONDS TO CONDENSE MY ENTIRE OUTLOOK ON LIFE INTO ONE CHARMING AND POIGNANT COMMENT.

THE COMMERCIALS WEREN'T LONG ENOUGH!!
Guisewite

WANT ME TO PUT THESE IN THE DISHWASHER, CATHY?
NO. THE DISHES IN THE DISHWASHER ARE CLEAN.

CATHY, THERE ARE 2 CLEAN CUPS IN THE DISHWASHER AND 300 DIRTY DISHES ON THE COUNTER!!

ANDREA, I'VE GONE THIS LONG WITHOUT EMPTYING THE DISHWASHER. I'M NOT GOING TO BREAK DOWN NOW WHEN I'M SO CLOSE TO VICTORY.
I CAN'T BELIEVE THIS! HERE. I'LL EMPTY THE DISHWASHER.

SATISFIED?
NYAH NYAH NYAH NYAH NYAH!!
Guisewite

CHARLENE SPENT THE MORNING COMPLAINING ABOUT THE FACT THAT MORRIE NEVER CLEANS UP THE COFFEE ROOM.

THEN JOANN ACCUSED TIM OF STEALING HER IDEAS FOR THE DRAPE PROJECT... THEN BETH ANNOUNCED SHE WAS GOING TO QUIT IF SUE DIDN'T QUIT HOGGING THE WHITE-OUT.

NOW IT'S 4:30 AND YOU'VE BEEN WAITING TO HAVE A MEETING WITH ME ALL DAY... WHAT DID YOU WANT TO DISCUSS, MR. PINKLEY?

CARLA CALLED ME "FATTY"!!

WHY DON'T YOU EVER INVITE ME TO YOUR BUSINESS DINNERS, CATHY?

IRVING, HONEY, IF YOU CAME, I'D SPEND THE WHOLE EVENING WORRYING ABOUT WHETHER OR NOT YOU WERE ENJOYING YOURSELF.

"WHAT'S IRVING THINKING ABOUT?"... "DOES HE FEEL LEFT OUT?"... "IS HE THREATENED?"...
FORGET IT, CATHY. FORGET I EVEN BROUGHT IT UP!!

...WHAT'S IRVING THINKING ABOUT?... DOES HE FEEL LEFT OUT?... IS HE THREATENED?...

I KNOW IRVING AND I ARE TOTALLY DIFFERENT PEOPLE, ANDREA... BUT WE KEEP COMING BACK TO EACH OTHER.

DEEP DOWN, I THINK WE BOTH WANT EXACTLY THE SAME THING!

WE BOTH WANT THE OTHER PERSON TO CHANGE.

CATHY, THEY'VE HAD YOUR CAR FOR 4 DAYS. WHY AREN'T YOU SCREAMING AT THEM?!

IF YOU SCREAM AT THE SERVICE DEPARTMENT THEY PUT YOUR NAME AT THE BOTTOM OF THEIR LIST, ANDREA. BUT WATCH THIS...

HI THERE! HOW'S THE FAMILY? WHEN DO YOU THINK THAT MAGNIFICENT OIL CHANGE MIGHT BE DONE?
SEPTEMBER 22.

THE SERVICE DEPARTMENTS ARE CATCHING ON.

3 TABLESPOONS OF TUNA SALAD AT 193 CALORIES PER 4-OUNCE SERVING... PLUS 2/3 CUP COTTAGE CHEESE AT 260 CALORIES PER CUP... PLUS 1½ OLIVES AT 52 CALORIES PER OUNCE..

...MINUS JOGGING FOR 22 MINUTES, WHICH BURNS OFF 300 CALORIES PER HOUR... MINUS 13 SIT-UPS AT-200 CALORIES PER HOUR...

...EQUALS 21% OF THE MAXIMUM CALORIES ALLOWED TO LOSE WEIGHT AT A RATE OF 2 POUNDS PER WEEK.

WHO GETS THE BILL?
YOU HANDLE IT, ANDREA. I CAN NEVER FIGURE OUT THE TIP.

I'LL BE FINE, MOM. EVERYTHING WILL WORK OUT JUST FINE.

YOUR YOUTH IS SLIPPING AWAY, CATHY. IF YOU DON'T MAKE SOME DECISIONS SOON, THEY'LL BE MADE FOR YOU.
WAAAH! YOU'RE RIGHT! WHAT AM I DOING? WAAAH!!

OH, YOU'LL BE FINE, CATHY. EVERYTHING WILL WORK OUT JUST FINE.

YOU TRICKED ME.
I WAS FEELING LEFT OUT.

I'LL RUN OUT AND GET SOME CHARCOAL.
I'LL START THE SALAD...

OH, HI, ANDREA. IRVING AND I ARE HAVING A BARBEQUE.
IF YOU WANT YOUR LIFE TO ROT AWAY WHILE YOU WASTE ANOTHER DAY GRILLING HOT DOGS WITH THAT EGOTISTICAL PIG, THAT'S YOUR BUSINESS.

HI, CATHY. I'M BACK.

NEVER LEAVE IN THE MIDDLE OF A DATE.

DEAR CATHY...THANKS FOR YOUR EXCELLENT PRESENTATION. WE LOOK FORWARD TO WORKING WITH YOU.
DEAR MARK...THANKS FOR THE NOTE. WE ALL APPRECIATE YOUR TIME AND ENTHUSIASM.

DEAR CATHY...THANKS FOR THE NOTE. KEEP UP THE GOOD WORK, AND WE HOPE TO SEE YOU AGAIN SOON.
DEAR MARK...THANKS FOR THE NOTE. I HOPE BUSINESS IS GOING WELL.

DEAR CATHY...THANKS FOR THE NOTE. GIVE MY BEST TO EVERYONE AT PRODUCT TESTING, INC.

DEAR MARK...I PROMISE TO NOT WRITE ANY MORE THANK YOU NOTES IF YOU PROMISE TO NOT WRITE ANY MORE THANK YOU NOTES.

YOU'RE SO DEPENDABLE, CATHY. YOU'RE THE ONLY PERSON I CAN TURN TO FOR HELP.
IN

COULD YOU POSSIBLY HANDLE ALL OF MORRIE'S WORK WHILE HE'S ON VACATION?
YES, MR. PINKLEY. I BELIEVE I COULD DO THAT.
IN

YES! I CAN DO IT! I WILL DO IT!! YES! I WILL HANDLE IT ALL!!!
IN

WHAT HAPPENED IN HERE?
I JUST TRADED 2 SECONDS OF OMNIPOTENCE FOR 2 WEEKS OF GRIEF.
IN

IRVING HONEY, I HAVE TO BREAK OUR DATE FOR TOMORROW NIGHT.

IRVING, MY DARLING HONEY, I HAVE TO BREAK OUR DATE FOR TOMORROW NIGHT.

IRVING, MY DARLING HONEY, WONDERFUL, PRECIOUS SWEETIE, I...

THE LONGER I DON'T SAY ANYTHING, THE BETTER YOU GET.
GUISEWITE

I'VE BEEN CALLED OUT OF TOWN ON BUSINESS. I NEED MY CLOTHES BACK.
YOU JUST BROUGHT THOSE IN AN HOUR AGO.
24-HOUR DRY CLEANING
GUISEWITE

I KNOW. BUT NOW I NEED THEM BACK.
YOU CAN'T HAVE THEM BACK. THEY'RE FILTHY AND THEY'RE WADDED UP IN A BAG.

GIVE ME BACK MY FILTHY, WADDED-UP CLOTHES!!
FOR WHAT?

I HAVE TO LOOK NICE IN A MEETING.

YOU SHOULD HAVE CHECKED THAT BAG, MISS. IT WON'T FIT UNDER YOUR SEAT.
IT FIT UNDER THE SEAT IN OTHER AIRPLANES.

IT WON'T FIT UNDER THE SEAT.
I BET I CAN MAKE IT FIT IF I JUMP ON IT.

MISS, WILL YOU AND YOUR TRUNK GET OUT OF THE AISLE? 200 PASSENGERS ARE WAITING BEHIND YOU.

SOME PEOPLE HAVE NO CONSIDERATION.
GUISEWITE

ROOM SERVICE.
HI. I'D LIKE TO ORDER BREAKFAST. HOW LONG WILL IT TAKE?
HOTEL DIRECTORY

THAT DEPENDS. IF YOU ORDER NOW, WE'LL DELIVER IT WHEN YOU'RE RIGHT IN THE MIDDLE OF YOUR SHOWER.
HOTEL
ROOM SERVICE

HOWEVER, IF YOU ORDER BREAKFAST AFTER YOUR SHOWER, WE'LL WAIT TO BRING IT UNTIL 4 SECONDS BEFORE YOU HAVE TO LEAVE FOR YOUR MEETING.
ROOM SERVICE

COULDN'T YOU JUST PLAN TO BRING IT 20 MINUTES FROM NOW?
DON'T BE RIDICULOUS. WE CAN'T TIME THINGS THAT EXACTLY.
ROOM SERVICE
Guisewite

THANKS FOR DINNER AND FOR NOT TRYING TO KISS ME, RALPH.
NO PROBLEM. I HAVE A WHOLE NEW RESPECT FOR MY FEMALE BUSINESS ASSOCIATES.
HOTEL

YOU MADE ME REALIZE HOW TACKY IT IS TO EXPECT A KISS IN RETURN FOR BUYING YOU A $50 BUSINESS DINNER.

INSTEAD, YOU CAN REPAY ME BY GIVING AN INFORMAL 45-MINUTE TALK TO 50 OF OUR SALES PEOPLE AT 8:00 TOMORROW MORNING.

EVERY NOW AND THEN, I HATE PROGRESS.
HOTEL
Guisewite

HI, CATHY. HOW'S YOUR TRIP?
AT 10:00 TONIGHT MY CLIENT TOLD ME I WAS SUPPOSED TO GIVE A 45-MINUTE TALK AT 8:00 TOMORROW MORNING, ANDREA.

THEY ONLY GAVE ME ONE NIGHT TO PREPARE A 45-MINUTE TALK FOR 50 PEOPLE!!

ONE NIGHT TO PREPARE WHAT COULD BE THE MOST IMPORTANT PRESENTATION OF MY ENTIRE CAREER!!
OH, CATHY... WHAT ARE YOU GOING TO DO?!

I DECIDED TO GET UP EARLY AND DO IT IN THE MORNING.
Guisewite

ALL SET FOR YOUR BIG TALK, CATHY?
YESTERDAY YOU SAID IT WAS AN "INFORMAL CHAT".

WHAT HAPPENED DURING THE NIGHT THAT TURNED IT INTO A "BIG TALK"?
OH, IT ALWAYS WAS A BIG TALK.

WE DIDN'T WANT YOU TO WORRY SO WE CALLED IT AN "INFORMAL CHAT." WHAT HAVE YOU PREPARED IN THE WAY OF AN OPENING?

YAAAA!!
CATCHY.
Guisewite

YOU LOOK EXHAUSTED, CATHY.
EXHAUSTED BUT TRIUMPHANT, ANDREA.
BAGGAGE CLAIM

MY PRESENTATION WAS BRILLIANT. I WAS POISED, PROFESSIONAL AND A TRIBUTE TO THE DYNAMIC NEW WOMAN OF THE '80s!

NOW ALL I WANT TO DO IS GO HOME AND LIE DOWN...
365

...NEXT TO MY OWN BED.
Guisewite

IF YOU GIVE ME YOUR RECEIPTS, I'LL DO YOUR EXPENSE REPORT, CATHY.
THANKS, CHARLENE. THE FIRST DAY OF THE TRIP, I RECORDED EVERY CENT I SPENT IN MY EXPENSE LOG BOOK.

THE SECOND DAY OF THE TRIP I KEPT ALL RECEIPTS IN THE SAME COMPARTMENT OF MY PURSE.

THE THIRD DAY I CRAMMED RECEIPTS ANYWHERE I FELT LIKE IT, AND SOMETIMES I DIDN'T EVEN KEEP THEM AT ALL!!

WHAT DO YOU EXPECT ME TO DO WITH ALL THIS??
THANK THE HEAVENS I WASN'T GONE TWO WEEKS.
Guisewite

IS THIS THE WARRANTY REGISTRATION CARD YOU'RE SUPPOSED TO SEND IN FOR YOUR PHONE-ANSWERING MACHINE, CATHY ?
YES, MOM. HERE. IT GOES IN THIS DRAWER.

YOU STUFF YOUR WARRANTY REGISTRATION CARDS IN A DRAWER ??
WHAT DO YOU DO WITH YOURS ?

I LET THEM SIT ON THE COUNTER UNTIL I SPILL SOMETHING ON THEM, AND THEN I THROW THEM OUT.

EVERY GENERATION HAS HER OWN SYSTEM.
Guisewite

PLEASE LEAVE A SHORT MESSAGE AFTER THE BEEP...BEEP!
HI. IT'S IRVING...UM... I HAD A GREAT TIME LAST NIGHT AND I..UH.. WELL, UM...I MISS YOU..I.

IRVING, WAIT! MY DARLING! I'M HERE ! I'M...
YAAA! YOU WERE LISTENING IN!!

YAAA! YOU LISTENED! FORGET EVERYTHING I SAID! YAAA !! *CLICK*

...ANOTHER MODERN CONVENIENCE BACKFIRES IN APARTMENT 365.
Guisewite

WE'RE FREEZING, MR. PINKLEY.

IT'S 100° OUTSIDE AND 52° IN THIS OFFICE. WE'RE TOO COLD TO WORK AND WE'RE SICK OF HIDING OUR LOVELY SUMMER OUTFITS UNDER THESE UGLY COATS.

EITHER TURN OFF THE AIR-CONDITIONER OR THE WOMEN IN THIS OFFICE ARE GOING TO MARCH OUT INTO THE SUNSHINE AND YOU CAN...

...HM! I SEEM TO BE WARMING UP.
Guisewite

I PAID $14.95 FOR THIS DOUBLE ALBUM SET AND I HATE EVERY SONG ON IT BUT ONE.

I'M GOING TO SMASH IT TO PIECES!
CATHY, NO! TAKE IT BACK TO THE RECORD STORE AND MAKE THEM DEAL WITH IT.

HELLO. I PAID $14.95 FOR THAT DOUBLE ALBUM SET AND I HATE EVERY SONG ON IT BUT ONE!!
SMASH!

SEE HOW MUCH MORE SATISFYING IT IS TO WORK WITHIN THE SYSTEM?
Guisewite

I CAN'T TAKE IT, MR. PINKLEY! I'M CRACKING UNDER ALL THIS WORK!!
OH, CATHY. LET ME HELP YOU.

LET'S SEE... YOU HAVE THE DRAPE UPDATE DUE. IS THAT THE PROBLEM?... THERE'S THE McMEEL RESEARCH. THAT DOESN'T LOOK SO BAD...
OH, NO YOU DON'T, MR. PINKLEY.
PINKLEY

YOU'RE PURPOSELY BREAKING MY WORKLOAD INTO TINY PIECES SO EACH ONE WILL SEEM INSIGNIFICANT AND DIMINISH THE IMPACT OF THE WHOLE.
PINKLEY

HOW DID YOU KNOW THAT?
IT'S THE SAME WAY I EAT A PIE.
PINKLEY
Guisewite

YOU LOOK FINE AS YOU ARE.
IT WILL JUST TAKE A SECOND TO CHANGE, IRVING.

...IT'S BEEN 35 MINUTES. I SHOULD LOOK BETTER THAN THIS IF I SPENT 35 MINUTES ON IT.

YAAA! NOW IT'S BEEN 45 MINUTES. HE'S GOING TO BE EXPECTING A MIRACLE AFTER WAITING 45 MINUTES!

CATHY, IT'S BEEN AN HOUR AND A HALF! WHAT ARE YOU DOING IN THERE?!
GO HOME, IRVING.
Guisewite

DEAR FLOYD,
WE ARE SICK AND TIRED OF YOUR OUTRAGEOUS DEMANDS. AS FAR AS I'M CONCERNED, YOU CAN TAKE YOUR BUSINESS AND...

DEAR FLOYD,
THIS IS THE LAST TIME PRODUCT TESTING INC. IS GOING TO CATER TO ONE OF YOUR LUDICROUS EMERGENCIES. IN THE...

DEAR FLOYD,
ENCLOSED ARE THE PROJECTS YOU REQUESTED.
BEST WISHES,
CATHY.

A GOOD BUSINESS LETTER TAKES SEVERAL DRAFTS.
Guisewite

I'M LOST.
WHAT DO YOU MEAN, YOU'RE LOST, CATHY?

I DON'T KNOW WHERE I BELONG, ANDREA. I'M WITH A PERSON FOR A WHILE, AND THEN I JUST FEEL LOST AGAIN.

EVEN WHEN PEOPLE SAY, "I NEVER WANT TO LOSE YOU," I ALWAYS WIND UP FEELING LOST.

THIS MUST BE WHAT IT FEELS LIKE TO BE A PAIR OF SUNGLASSES.
Guisewite

WHAT DO YOU WANT TO DO IN THE NEXT FIVE YEARS, CATHY?
YOU WERE ALWAYS ON MY MIND... YOU WERE ALWAYS ON MY MIND...

I WOULD LIKE TO SPEND THE NEXT FIVE YEARS STARING AT YOUR GORGEOUS FACE.
I'M SORRY... I COULDN'T HEAR YOU OVER THE MUSIC.
TELL ME THAT YOUR SWEET LOVE HAS NOT DIED...

UM... I'D LIKE TO SPEND THE NEXT FIVE YEARS EXPLORING THE MANY FASCINATING ASPECTS OF MY CAREER.
OH.

ANOTHER RELATIONSHIP GETS DROWNED OUT BY A LOVE SONG.
Guisewite

HA, HA, HA!...OH, YOU'RE WONDERFUL! WHAT A WONDERFUL TIME I HAD WITH YOU TONIGHT, NICK.

I FIND YOU JUST FASCINATING. FASCINATING, HANDSOME AND WONDERFUL!!

I CAN'T REMEMBER ENJOYING A DATE MORE! THANK YOU, YOU CHARMING, HANDSOME GENTLEMAN!!
YOU'RE WELCOME. GOODNIGHT, CATHY.

MAYBE HE DOESN'T KNOW I LIKE HIM.
Guisewite

WHAT MAKES YOU THINK I MET SOMEONE NEW?
YOU'RE WEARING THAT SPARKLY PURPLE STUFF ON YOUR EYELIDS.

I'VE WORN THIS EYESHADOW BEFORE, IRVING.
YOU'RE WEARING NAVY BLUE MASCARA AND THREE DIFFERENT COLORS OF EYELINER.

THE ONLY TIME YOU LOOK LIKE THAT IS RIGHT AFTER YOU'VE MET SOMEONE NEW, WHEN YOU FEEL CONFIDENT ENOUGH TO TRY SOMETHING WEIRD WITH YOUR MAKE-UP!

HOW DID IRVING FIND OUT ABOUT NICK?
HE SAID HE COULD SEE IT IN MY EYES.
Guisewite

I NEED A GOOD TRAVELING DRESS. ARE YOU SURE THIS ONE WON'T WRINKLE?
OH, NO. THAT MATERIAL NEVER WRINKLES.

WAD WAD

WRINKLE
WAD
WRINKLE
WAD
CRUMPLE
WRINKLE WRINKLE

YOU PUT IT ON WRONG.
Guisewite

I'M REALLY GLAD I MET YOU, CATHY.
OH, ME TOO, NICK!

I'VE HARDLY EVER HAD WOMEN IN MY LIFE WHO WERE REALLY **FRIENDS**.

IT'S SUCH A TREAT FOR MEN AND WOMEN TO BE ABLE TO SPEND TIME TOGETHER **JUST AS FRIENDS**!
YES, YES. ISN'T IT WONDERFUL?

Guisewite

YOU'RE WONDERFUL, NICK.
CATHY...UM... I'M JUST NOT INTERESTED IN GETTING INVOLVED RIGHT NOW.. YOU UNDERSTAND, DON'T YOU?

YES NICK... BY SAYING THAT, YOU'RE GIVING ME A GRACEFUL WAY OUT OF THIS RELATIONSHIP WITHOUT FURTHER HUMILIATING MYSELF BY THROWING MYSELF AT YOUR FEET.

...YOU'RE EVEN MORE WONDERFUL THAN I THOUGHT!!
Guisewite

TO NICK, WHO HAD HIS BIG CHANCE AND BLEW IT!
TO PHIL, WHO RAN OFF WITH MY SISTER!

TO TONY, WHO RUINED MY LIFE!

TO SWEET, ADORABLE FRANK, WHO ASKED ME TO BE HIS BRIDE!!

NOTHING RUINS LUNCH LIKE A PIECE OF GOOD NEWS.
Guisewite

YOU ALWAYS SAID YOU NEVER WANTED TO GET MARRIED, CHARLENE.
I CHANGED MY MIND.

FOR 4 YEARS YOU'VE COME INTO MY OFFICE BEFORE WORK AND GIVEN SPEECHES ON HOW YOU NEVER WANTED TO GET MARRIED.
WELL, I CHANGED MY MIND!

YOU SAT RIGHT HERE AND CHANGED MY WHOLE PERSPECTIVE ON MARRIAGE, CHARLENE. YOU SWORE YOU'D NEVER GET MARRIED!!

NEVER TRUST PROMISES PEOPLE MAKE WHEN THEY'RE EATING DONUTS.
IN
Guisewite

CATHY, JUST BECAUSE I'M GETTING MARRIED DOESN'T MEAN WE'LL QUIT BEING FRIENDS.

YOU CAN STILL TELL ME ABOUT YOUR PATHETIC DATES. ... AND I'LL TELL YOU ABOUT MY SWEET ADORABLE HUSBAND ... WE'LL STILL DRIVE TO SINGLE'S PLACES. I'LL JUST DROP YOU OFF AND RUSH HOME TO MY SWEET ADORABLE HUSBAND.
PLEASE CLEAN YOUR OWN ME

WE CAN EVEN DOUBLE DATE! YOU'LL BRING SOME MISERABLE STRANGER, AND I'LL BRING MY SWEET, ADORABLE HUSBAND!

SEE? OUR FRIENDSHIP WILL STAY EXACTLY THE SAME!!
WHAT A RELIEF.
CATHY
Guisewite

WHEN NICK SAID OUR RELATIONSHIP WAS HOPELESS, I CELEBRATED MY INDEPENDENCE BY BUYING A LOVELY NEW NECKLACE.

WHEN IRVING STOMPED OFF, I REAFFIRMED MY SELF-WORTH BY FINDING A GORGEOUS NEW DRESS.

WHEN MY BEST CLIENT CUT HIS BUDGET IN HALF, I EASED MY STRESS BY TAKING A HOT BUBBLE BATH, CURLING MY HAIR, AND MANICURING MY NAILS.

THE WORSE THINGS GET, THE BETTER I LOOK.
Guisewite

HOW COULD CHARLENE MARRY A MAN LIKE FRANK? I THOUGHT SHE'D MADE MORE PROGRESS THAN THAT.
SALE

CATHY, FRANK IS EXACTLY THE TYPE OF GUY THAT IRVING IS, AND YOU'VE DATED HIM FOR 5 YEARS!
SALE

WHAT PROGRESS DO YOU THINK YOU'VE MADE ??

I'M LESS TOLERANT OF MY FRIENDS' RELATIONSHIPS.
GUSEWITZ

BZZZ
BZZZ
BZZZZZ
BZZZZ
YOU'RE STILL HERE ??

DON'T YOU HAVE ANYWHERE ELSE TO GO? DON'T YOU HAVE SOMETHING ELSE TO DO ??
BZZZ
BZZZZ
BZZZ

YOU HAVE THE WHOLE WORLD TO PICK FROM !! WHY ARE YOU TORTURING ME ??
BZZZZ
BZZZZZ
BZZZ

COMPANY ALWAYS STAYS TOO LONG IN AUGUST.
BZZZ
BZZZ
BZZZ
BZZZ
GUSEWITZ

IRVING.....
AACK. I CAN'T SAY THAT. I'LL SOUND SO CONFUSED AND WEAK.

I AM CONFUSED. BUT IT'S SO EMBARRASSING TO ADMIT IT. I'M SCARED TO SAY I CARE. I'M SCARED TO SAY I DON'T.

AAAGH. THIS IS AGONY! THIS IS TORTURE TO OPEN UP TO HIM...
IRVING, I THINK WE NEED TO DISCUSS OUR RELATIONSHIP.

SURE YOU DO. IT'S SO EASY FOR WOMEN TO TALK ABOUT THEIR FEELINGS.
GUSEWITZ

NICK DUMPED ME, MOM.
GOOD RIDDANCE, NICK, YOU MISERABLE SCUM!!!

HE WAS VERY NICE...
OH, NICK... WE MISS YOU, NICK!!

MAYBE HE FELT THREATENED BY IRVING.
PHOOEY ON YOU, IRVING! YOU RUIN EVERYTHING!!!

NO, THAT'S NOT IT. IRVING'S BEEN WONDERFUL...
YOU'RE GIVING YOUR MOTHER A HEADACHE, CATHY.

ONE HUNDRED AND... WAIT. I DON'T THINK THE SCALE WAS EXACTLY ON ZERO WHEN I GOT ON.

NOPE. IT WAS A TEENSY BIT OVER ZERO. THE SCALE MUST START **EXACTLY ON ZERO** OR THE READING ISN'T ACCURATE... NO, IT'S STILL A FRACTION OVER... NO... NO....

...THERE!
CATHY, THAT WAS AT LEAST 5 POUNDS **UNDER** ZERO WHEN YOU GOT ON!

I GOT TIRED OF TRYING TO FIX IT.

I WAS JUST IN A RELATIONSHIP WHERE I DID ALL THE WORK, IRVING. IT'S YOUR TURN.
MY TURN?? **I** WASN'T IN YOUR LAST RELATIONSHIP.

I KNOW... BUT IN THE BIG PICTURE OF MEN AND WOMEN, IT'S THE **MAN'S** TURN TO PUT OUT THE EFFORT AND **MY** TURN TO BE PAMPERED AND ADORED.
WHAT??

GO AHEAD, IRVING. FLATTER ME. CHARM ME. **BEG ME TO BE YOURS LIKE I BEGGED NICK TO BE MINE!!**
BLEAHHH!

WHERE'S IRVING?
THERE'S AN OUTSIDE CHANCE THAT HE WENT TO BUY ME A GIFT.

OUR MOTHERS JUST DIDN'T TALK ABOUT THINGS, CATHY.
I KNOW. WHEN MY MOM IS REALLY UPSET ONE OF HER FINGERS MOVES A LITTLE... BUT THAT'S IT.
Coffee to go

THEY WERE CONDITIONED TO KEEP EVERYTHING INSIDE.
HER WHOLE RAGE ON A SUBJECT COMES OUT AS ONE TINY, NERVOUS MOVE OF ONE FINGER.

THANK HEAVENS OUR GENERATION IS BEYOND THAT!
HOORAY FOR US!!

WE'VE LEARNED TO USE OUR ENTIRE HAND.
Guisewite

I READ A STORY ABOUT A WOMAN MY AGE WHO STARTED A COMPANY AND IS MAKING $200,000 A YEAR. I RAN HOME AND ATE A BOX OF DONUTS.
donuts

I TALKED TO A FRIEND WHO'S GROVELLING AROUND TRYING TO FIGURE OUT WHAT TO DO WITH HER LIFE. I CHARGED OVER TO MY OFFICE AND FINISHED 4 PROJECTS.
OUT
IN

WHEN SALLY WAS MADE A VICE PRESIDENT, I ATE A CARTON OF COOL-WHIP...
...WHEN PAM GOT FIRED, I WROTE A BRILLIANT, 20-PAGE RESEARCH REPORT.
COOL-WHIP

I'M RESPONDING TO ALL THE WRONG ROLE MODELS.
Guisewite

ARE YOU SURE YOU CAN'T STAY FOR AWHILE, IRVING? MY MOTHER BROUGHT OVER THIS GREAT PIE.
NO... I'D BETTER GET GOING, CATHY.

ARE YOU SURE? IT'S JUST DELICIOUS, AND THERE'S A GREAT MOVIE ON LATER.
NO. THANKS, BUT I REALLY HAVE TO GO.

CATHY, IT'S ME. I CHANGED MY MIND.
KNOCK KNOCK
Guisewite

I CLEANED UP THE KITCHEN LAST NIGHT! OH, WHAT A BEAUTIFUL SIGHT!

HALLELUJAH! MY KITCHEN IS CLEAN!

THERE IS NOTHING MORE WONDERFUL THAN A CLEAN KITCHEN IN THE MORNING!!!

...WITH THE POSSIBLE EXCEPTION OF A CLEAN BATHROOM.
Guisewite

IS SOMETHING WRONG, TIM?
I'M SORRY, SUE. THAT SONG REMINDS ME OF MY OLD GIRL-FRIEND, JULIE.

IS SOMETHING WRONG, SUE?
I'M SORRY, JAY. THAT SONG REMINDS ME OF TIM BECAUSE IT REMINDS HIM OF JULIE.

IS SOMETHING WRONG, JAY?
I'M SORRY, CATHY. THAT SONG REMINDS ME OF SUE BECAUSE IT REMINDS HER OF TIM. IT REMINDS TIM OF JULIE.

IS SOMETHING WRONG, CATHY?
WHY IS EVERYTHING SO COMPLICATED BY THE TIME IT GETS TO ME?
Guisewite

WHEN DO YOU THINK YOU COULD GET THIS PROJECT DONE, CATHY?
FEBRUARY, 1983.
PINKLEY

FEBRUARY! HA, HA! WHAT A KIDDER! THE CLIENT NEEDS IT FRIDAY!
FRIDAY! HA, HA! THAT'S A GOOD ONE, MR. PINKLEY! TRY APRIL, 1983!
PINKLEY

APRIL! HOO, HA! HE'LL BE HERE AT 8:00 SHARP FRIDAY MORNING!
8:00! HA, HA! OH, YOU'RE TOO MUCH!! 8:00! HOO, HA!

NEVER TRUST A LAUGHING BOSS.
PINKLEY
Guisewite

YOU'RE WORKING LATE? YOU PROMISED YOU'D HELP PLAN MY DINNER PARTY.
I'M SORRY, MOM. NEXT WEEK I'LL COOK THE WHOLE DINNER AND HELP YOU CLEAN YOUR ENTIRE HOUSE.

YOU'RE WORKING LATE? WHAT ABOUT THE PAMPHLETS YOU SAID YOU'D HELP ME MAIL?
I'M SORRY, ANDREA. NEXT WEEK I'LL HAND-DELIVER THE PAMPHLETS WITH A PERSONAL NOTE OF APOLOGY TO EACH ONE.

YOU'RE WORKING LATE? I THOUGHT WE WERE GOING TO SEE A MOVIE.
I'M SORRY, IRVING. NEXT WEEK I'LL TAKE YOU TO EVERY MOVIE IN TOWN AND I'LL WAX YOUR CAR.

...JUST THINK, CATHY. WHEN THIS WEEK IS OVER, YOU CAN JUST SIT BACK AND RELAX!
GUISEWITE

IF YOU DON'T GET THE PROJECT DONE, YOU'LL UNDERMINE YOUR CLIENT'S TRUST AND RISK LOSING THE BUSINESS THAT PAYS YOUR SALARY, CATHY.

THEN AGAIN, IF YOU DO GET THE PROJECT DONE, YOU'LL HAVE SET A PRECEDENT FOR SPEED THAT WILL HAUNT YOU THE REST OF YOUR CAREER AND GIVE YOU A NERVOUS BREAKDOWN.

IF YOU GET THE PROJECT DONE BUT DO IT POORLY BECAUSE YOU'RE HURRYING, YOU'LL DEMEAN YOUR CAPABILITIES AND DESTROY ALL CHANCE FOR ADVANCEMENT.

I LOVE A JOB WITH AN ELEMENT OF SUSPENSE.
GUISEWITE

WELL, HERE WE ALL ARE: COFFEE TO HELP ME STAY AWAKE... COOKIES TO HELP ME WRITE...
CATHY

DONUTS TO HELP ME TYPE... PRETZELS TO HELP ME PROOF-READ... CHOCOLATE TO HELP ME COLLATE...
CATHY

CATHY

HOW'S IT GOING, CATHY?
MY STAFF KEEPS DISAPPEARING.
CATHY
GUISEWITE

YOU'RE STILL IN THE SHOWER?
I CAN'T REMEMBER WHICH BLADES ARE NEW AND WHICH ONES ARE USED, ANDREA.

CATHY, YOU'RE GOING TO MAKE US BOTH LATE.
HERE. THIS ONE'S GOOD...YAAK! NO IT ISN'T..OUCH! YAAK! THEY ALL LOOK THE SAME!

CATHY, FOR HEAVEN'S SAKE. WHY DON'T YOU JUST WEAR SLACKS TODAY?
I HAVE A VERY BIG MEETING THIS MORNING, ANDREA.

IT'S IMPORTANT FOR ME TO LOOK FEMININE.
Guisewite

YOUR PRESENTATION WAS WONDERFUL, CATHY.
FLATTERY IS NOT GOING TO BUY ME OFF THIS TIME, MR. PINKLEY.

YOU DID A FANTASTIC JOB.
NO ONE IN THIS COMPANY WOULD HAVE PUT UP WITH WHAT YOU EXPECTED OF ME THIS WEEK.

IT WAS BRILLIANT!
I DO 10 TIMES MORE WORK FOR A FRACTION OF THE PAY AND THEN YOU GLOSS OVER IT ALL WITH A FEW KIND WORDS!

MR. PINKLEY...
NOT NOW, CHARLENE. I'M SCREAMING AT HIM FOR COMPLIMENTING ME.
Guisewite

WHAT'S THE DIFFERENCE? IT'S ONLY ONE EVENING OF MY LIFE.
NOW PLAYING

... NO, THAT'S TERRIBLE. I SHOULDN'T BE HERE IF I HAVE ABSOLUTELY NO INTEREST IN THIS PERSON.

...NO, THAT'S WRONG. IT'S GOOD FOR ME TO GO OUT WITH DIFFERENT TYPES OF PEOPLE. I NEED THE EXPERIENCE.

YOU'VE BEEN SO QUIET ALL EVENING, CATHY...
I'M STILL TRYING TO DECIDE WHETHER OR NOT I SHOULD GO OUT WITH YOU TONIGHT.
Guisewite

SHOULD I CALL IRVING OR NOT, ANDREA? WHAT DO YOU THINK?

CATHY, WHY DO YOU MAKE YOURSELF CRAZY GETTING EVERYONE'S OPINION ON EVERYTHING?

FOR ONCE, WHY DON'T YOU JUST ASK THE ONE AND ONLY PERSON WHOSE OPINION COUNTS??

HELLO, IRVING? SHOULD I CALL YOU OR NOT?
Guisewite

YOU WANT ME AROUND UNTIL YOU READ SOME WOMEN'S ARTICLE, AND THEN ALL YOU CARE ABOUT IS YOUR CAREER.

THEN YOU GET DISILLUSIONED BY YOUR CAREER AND YOU SEARCH FOR SOME BIG ROMANCE TO GIVE MEANING TO YOUR LIFE...YOU DATE YO-YO S.. ..YOU BEG ME TO COME BACK...

I COME BACK...I "THREATEN YOUR SPACE"... YOU THROW ME OUT... YOU DON'T KNOW WHAT YOU WANT, CATHY!!

...AT LAST! A MAN WHO REALLY UNDERSTANDS ME!
Guisewite

THAT'S A NEW KIND OF SUGAR-FREE SODA I GOT, CATHY. WHAT DO YOU THINK?

SWISH
SWISH
SWISH
SWISH
SWISH
MOUTH WASH

HM! NO AFTERTASTE.
diet
Guisewite

MY CAR SEATS LEAN ALL THE WAY BACK. ALMOST LIKE A BED.
HM. WHAT A LOVELY CHOCOLATE COLOR.

THIS SOFA IS A HIDEAWAY. YOU BELIEVE IT? THIS BEAUTY TURNS INTO A BED!
WHAT AN INTERESTING PATTERN. LIKE MILLIONS OF LITTLE OREOS.

OF COURSE, THIS CHAIR IS AS COMFORTABLE AS A BED! THERE'S ROOM FOR 2 ON HERE!
WELL, LOOK AT THAT! THAT LEATHER IS THE EXACT HUE OF THE INSIDE OF A MILK DUD!

TWO ONE-TRACK MINDS ON DIFFERENT TRACKS.

HERE, SWEETIE. IF YOU FOLDED YOUR TOWELS LIKE THIS, YOUR LINEN CLOSET WOULD BE SO MUCH MORE EFFICIENT!
I LIKE THE WAY I DO IT, MOTHER.

YOU COULD ALWAYS KEEP YOUR BILLS IN THIS LITTLE BASKET, AND THEN THEY WOULDN'T GET STREWN ALL OVER THE HOUSE!
I HAVE MY OWN SYSTEM, MOTHER.

ARRANGE PACKAGED PRODUCTS BY DATE OF PURCHASE, AND YOU'LL ALWAYS KNOW WHAT'S FRESH!
I'M A GROWN WOMAN! I DON'T NEED YOU TO TELL ME HOW TO RUN MY HOUSE!

WHAT'S WRONG WITH THIS SOAP, CATHY?
IT ISN'T THE KIND MY MOM ALWAYS BUYS.

NICE PARTY, HUH?
IT WAS HORRIBLE! WHENEVER SUE FEELS JEALOUS OF MY JOB, SHE GETS BACK BY THROWING HERSELF AT YOU LIKE THAT.

SUE WAS THROWING HERSELF AT ME??
OH, COME ON, IRVING... PLUS, BILL WASN'T SPEAKING TO JAN, SO JAN SPENT THE NIGHT FLIRTING WITH SUE'S BOYFRIEND, JOE.

YOU'RE KIDDING! I DIDN'T SEE THAT!
HOW ABOUT WHEN BILL'S OLD GIRLFRIEND SHOWED UP WITH HER NEW HUSBAND, WHO I USED TO DATE?

IT WAS ONE OF THE MOST TENSE, EMBARRASSING, AWKWARD EVENINGS OF MY LIFE!
WOMEN ALWAYS HAVE A BETTER TIME AT THESE THINGS THAN MEN DO.

THIS IS THE HOT NEW LOOK IN TWEEDY JACKETS FOR FALL...
FALL FASHION HEADS

AND THIS IS THE HOT NEW LOOK IN SKIRTS...
FALL FASHI HEAD

... PUT THEM TOGETHER WITH THE HOT NEW LOOK IN SWEATERS AND TEXTURED HOSE. IT'S HOT, HOT, HOT!

...BOY, DO YOU LOOK HOT, CATHY!
THANK YOU.
TICKETS

MORE SHOES? WHAT DO YOU NEED MORE SHOES FOR, CATHY?

THAT SEEMS A LITTLE RIDICULOUS COMING FROM A MAN WHO OWNS 132 SHIRTS, IRVING.

...NOT TO MENTION THE FACT THAT MEN'S SHIRTS ESSENTIALLY STAY IN STYLE FOR YEARS, WHEREAS WOMEN'S SHOES CHANGE RADICALLY EACH SEASON... THE QUALITY AND CUT OF WHICH ARE OFTEN THE BASIS BY WHICH A WOMAN'S ENTIRE PRESENCE IS JUDGED!

I HATE IT WHEN THE DEFENSE IS PREPARED.

I DON'T SEE WHY YOU WON'T LET ME FIX YOU UP, CATHY.
ANDREA, WAIT! DON'T EAT THAT TUNA SALAD! IT'S ROTTEN.

IF IT'S ROTTEN, WHAT'S IT DOING IN YOUR REFRIGERATOR?
WELL, IT'S NOT THAT ROTTEN... I MEAN, I'VE SORT OF GOTTEN USED TO SEEING IT IN THERE.

I COME HOME FROM WORK EVERY DAY AND THERE IT IS... A FAMILIAR FACE... A FRIEND... SOMEONE TO TALK..

ARE YOU SURE YOU DON'T WANT TO GET FIXED UP?
WHO EXACTLY DO YOU KNOW?

FLOYD AND HELEN, MARGO AND JACK, AND NEIMAN-MARCUS ARE CELEBRATING THEIR ANNIVERSARIES TODAY. I'M SENDING THEM ALL A NICE CARD.

NEIMAN-MARCUS IS A STORE, MOM.
THEY'VE BEEN TOGETHER 75 YEARS!

FOR 75 YEARS THEY'VE STAYED COMMITTED TO THEIR RELATIONSHIP, UNLIKE YOU YOUNG PEOPLE TODAY WHO BREAK UP BEFORE YOU EVEN KNOW EACH OTHER'S LAST NAMES!

I GET THE POINT, MOTHER.
POINT? WHAT POINT? I WAS JUST MAKING CONVERSATION.

WHY DID I TELL PINKLEY I'D WORK ON THAT STUPID PROJECT THIS WEEKEND??

WHY CAN'T I LOSE ANY WEIGHT? WHY AREN'T I SAVING ANY MONEY? WHY DO I LISTEN TO ANDREA'S ADVICE?

AND YOU, IRVING! WHY DO YOU ALWAYS DISAPPEAR JUST WHEN THINGS ARE STARTING TO WORK??

CLEANING THE HOUSE CAN BE VERY THERAPEUTIC.

MR. PINKLEY SAID YOU'D FILL ME IN ON THE NEW PERSON HE HIRED FOR MY DEPARTMENT.
HE'S SINGLE, CATHY! SINGLE, SINGLE, SINGLE!!

CHARLENE, THIS IS BUSINESS. COULD YOU POSSIBLY GIVE ME A LITTLE MORE USEFUL INFORMATION??
SORRY.

HE'S 5'10", WITH A POWERFUL YET LEAN WARREN BEATTY BODY, A PAUL SIMON SMILE, A TUMBLE OF SUN-STREAKED WALNUT HAIR, AND EYES THE COLOR OF A 1979 STEEL BLUE MERCEDES BENZ 450 SL.

THANK YOU.

CATHY, I'D LIKE YOU TO MEET GRANT. HE'LL BE WORKING DIRECTLY UNDER YOU.
HEE HEE

WHAT IS THE MATTER WITH ME ??

BLEEBLE BLEEBLE HEE HEE HEE
NICE MEETING YOU TOO, CATHY.

A NEW WORLD RECORD: FIVE YEARS OF PROGRESS, DOWN THE DRAIN IN FOUR SECONDS.

WHO ARE YOU ALL DOLLED-UP FOR, CATHY? YOUR NEW ASSISTANT, GRANT ???

CHARLENE, IF YOU EVEN HINT TO GRANT THAT I USUALLY DON'T LOOK THIS NICE, THE ENTIRE OFFICE IS GOING TO HEAR ABOUT YOU AND THE WORD PROCESSOR MAINTENANCE MAN.
RECEPTION

OPEN YOUR MOUTH ABOUT THAT MAINTENANCE MAN AND PINKLEY'S GOING TO KNOW WHO STEALS THE FIG NEWTONS FROM HIS TOP DRAWER.
ONE WORD ABOUT THOSE FIG NEWTONS AND I GO STRAIGHT TO YOUR FIANCÉ WITH...

NEVER MIND.
THERE'S NOTHING LIKE NEGOTIATING A BIG DEAL BEFORE 8:30 IN THE MORNING.

I'M STARVING. WANT TO GET SOME LUNCH, CATHY.?
UM... I DON'T THINK IT'S A GOOD IDEA, GRANT.
IN

DID YOU ALREADY EAT ?
NO, BUT IF I LEAVE THE OFFICE WITH YOU, EVERYONE WILL ASSUME IT'S A DATE.
IN

BELIEVE ME, THE SICK, CONTRIVING MINDS IN THIS OFFICE WILL TURN AN INNOCENT TUNA SANDWICH BETWEEN YOU AND ME INTO THE ROMANCE OF THE CENTURY !!
IN

WHO WOULD DO SOMETHING LIKE THAT ?
I WOULD.
IN

THERE ARE 7 MILLION MORE SINGLE ADULT WOMEN IN THIS COUNTRY THAN THERE ARE SINGLE ADULT MEN.

I SPEND 99% OF MY LIFE AT WORK. HOWEVER, I'M NOT SUPPOSED TO DATE ANYONE IN MY COMPANY.

WHAT, THEN, IS MY CHANCE OF MEETING AN AVAILABLE, ATTRACTIVE MAN IN MY 1% OF REMAINING TIME WHO SHARES AN INTEREST IN THE THINGS I DO, YET WORKS IN A TOTALLY DIFFERENT FIELD?

... I ALWAYS KNEW THOSE STORY PROBLEMS WOULD COME BACK TO HAUNT ME.
Guisewite

YESTERDAY GRANT SAID THE...
CATHY, FORGET GRANT. YOU ARE NOT GOING TO DATE SOMEONE WHO WORKS IN YOUR OFFICE.

DO YOU REALIZE HOW HIDEOUS IT WOULD BE IF YOU AND GRANT BROKE UP AND YOU STILL HAD TO SEE HIM EVERY DAY??

I BROKE UP WITH IRVING 5 YEARS AGO, AND I STILL SEE HIM EVERY DAY.

I REST MY CASE.
Guisewite

I'M GLAD YOU CHANGED YOUR MIND ABOUT DATING SOMEONE AT WORK.
THIS ISN'T A DATE, GRANT. WE'RE SITTING IN MY OFFICE.

CATHY, IT'S 9:00 AT NIGHT, WE'RE EATING DINNER, BRUCE SPRINGSTEEN IS SINGING IN THE BACKGROUND, AND WE'RE TALKING ABOUT THE PEOPLE WE'RE GOING TO GO OUT WITH.

YES, AND UNFORTUNATELY, SINCE WE'RE NOT GETTING ANYTHING DONE, WE'RE GOING TO HAVE TO WORK LATE AGAIN TOMORROW NIGHT!

OH, DARN.
DARN, DARN DARN...
Guisewite

YOU'RE FINALLY CLEANING OUT THIS CLOSET ??
WELL, I THOUGHT, WHAT IF GRANT ASKS ME OUT AND I SAY "YES".

THEN WHAT IF WE HAVE SUCH A WONDERFUL TIME THAT HE BEGS TO COME OVER AND FIX ME DINNER THIS WEEK-END... AND WHILE HE COOKS, I LEAN OVER AND WHISPER ENDEARING THINGS IN HIS EAR...

FLUSTERED BY MY COOL CHARM, HE KNOCKS THE HOLLANDAISE SAUCE ON THE FLOOR AND GOES LOOKING FOR A RAG TO CLEAN IT UP... IF THAT HAPPENED, I WOULD WANT THIS CLOSET TO BE NICE AND NEAT.

THIS IS PATHETIC, CATHY.
IT'S GETTING THE CLOSET CLEAN, ISN'T IT ?
Guisewite

SOMEONE FROM THE OFFICE IS GOING TO SEE US HERE, GRANT.
YOU'RE SO PARANOID, CATHY.

YOU'RE NOT PARANOID ?
CATHY, I DON'T CARE WHAT ANYONE IN THE OFFICE THINKS.

SO WHAT IF THEY SEE US ?? LET THEM SEE US ! LOOK !! CATHY AND GRANT ARE...
EXCUSE ME...

READY TO ORDER, SWEETHEART ?
Guisewite

WHAT MAKES YOU SUCH AN EXPERT ON DATING SOMEONE AT THE OFFICE, MOM ?
I SAW IT ON THE PHIL DONAHUE SHOW.

PHIL POINTED OUT THAT OFFICE DATING PUTS A HIDEOUS STRAIN ON BOTH YOUR WORK AND RELATIONSHIP, AND THE AUDIENCE CHEERED !

THEN PHIL SAID, "BUT COULDN'T A LOVING, DISCREET COUPLE MAKE IT WORK ?", AND THE AUDIENCE CHEERED THAT... THEN PHIL GOT EXASPERATED BECAUSE THE SAME PEOPLE KEPT CHEERING FOR OPPOSITE THINGS, AND THE AUDIENCE CHEERED THAT ! THEN...

WHAT'S YOUR POINT, MOM ?
I FORGOT.
Guisewite

THIS REPORT YOU DID IS ALL WRONG, GRANT... WELL, IT ISN'T THAT WRONG. NO. YES, IT IS. IT'S WRONG.

GRANT, I CAN'T DO THIS. WE ARE NOT GOING OUT ANYMORE. YOU HAVE TO RE-DO THIS WORK AND FORGET ABOUT GOING OUT.

WE ARE NEVER GOING OUT AGAIN. DO YOU WANT TO GO OUT TONIGHT AND TALK ABOUT IT??

WHY DOES THE WOMAN ALWAYS HAVE TO BE THE STRONG ONE?
Guisewite

GRANT'S PHONE IS BUSY. THAT'S AN OMEN THAT I SHOULDN'T BE CALLING HIM.

MY HAIR IS TANGLED. THAT'S AN OMEN THAT I SHOULDN'T BE GOING OUT WITH HIM TODAY.

HE'S 3 MINUTES LATE, AN OMEN THAT THIS WHOLE RELATIONSHIP IS OUT OF SYNC.

IT'S POURING OUT, CATHY. MAYBE WE SHOULDN'T BE GOING TO THE GAME TODAY.
MEN ARE SO SUPERSTITIOUS.
Guisewite

I LOVE GETTING TO SEE YOU IN THE OFFICE EVERY DAY, CATHY.
ME TOO, GRANT. BUT NO ONE ELSE CAN FIND OUT ABOUT US.
CATHY

NO ONE ELSE WILL EVER KNOW.
WE'LL GO OUT AT NIGHT, BUT AT THE OFFICE IT'S STRICTLY BUSINESS!

THEY'LL NEVER EVEN SUSPECT WE'RE DATING!
OH, GRANT! IT WILL BE OUR OWN BEAUTIFUL SECRET!!

Guisewite

LAURA WAS BEAUTIFUL... I WANT TO MEET SOMEONE AS BEAUTIFUL AS LAURA, AND AS BRIGHT AS MAUREEN.
I'M BEAUTIFUL. I'M BRIGHT.

I WANT SOMEONE AS WITTY AS JOAN, AS SENSITIVE AS KAREN, AS CHARMING AS SUE.
I'M WITTY. I'M SENSITIVE. I'M CHARMING.

I WANT...
ME! WHAT ABOUT ME? YOU IDIOT! ME! ME!!

NAH. TOO HYSTERICAL.
Guisewite

THIS IS WHAT MEN HATE, CATHY. I WENT WITH YOU A COUPLE OF TIMES, AND SUDDENLY YOU'RE MAKING ME FEEL THE PRESSURE OF A WHOLE RELATIONSHIP.

WE DON'T HAVE A RELATIONSHIP. WE HAD TWO GREAT DATES. WHO KNOWS? MAYBE WE'LL GO OUT AGAIN.

BUT UNTIL WE DO, I AM NOT GOING TO KISS THE GROUND YOU WALK ON, OR FEEL SOME HUGE GUILT BECAUSE I'M NOT DANCING THROUGH EVERY MOMENT OF MY LIFE WITH YOU!

WHAT DID GRANT SAY?
"GREAT DATES. GO OUT AGAIN. KISS AND DANCE."
Guisewite

IN THE 70'S WE USED TO LEAP INTO LOVE BUT THEN DENY THAT WE WERE INVOLVED.

NOW IT'S THE 80'S. WE TALK ABOUT HOW MUCH WE WANT TO GET INVOLVED, BUT WE STAY A MILE AWAY FROM AN ACTUAL RELATIONSHIP.

WERE WE BETTER OFF CARING AND PRETENDING WE DION'T, OR ARE WE BETTER OFF ADMITTING WE WANT TO CARE, EVEN THOUGH WE RUN WHEN THE OPPORTUNITY PRESENTS ITSELF?

...THIS MAY BE A TWO-CAKE QUESTION.
Guisewite

WHAT WERE YOU DOING SO LATE AT THE OFFICE, CATHY?
WHY? ARE YOU JEALOUS, IRVING?

WHY? WOULD YOU LIKE IT IF I WERE JEALOUS?
WHY? IF I SAID I LIKED IT, WOULD YOU FEEL MANIPULATED?

WHY? IF I FELT MANIPULATED, WOULD YOU ACCUSE ME OF OVER-REACTING?
WHY? IF I SAID YOU OVER-REACTED, WOULD YOU TAKE ME IN YOUR ARMS AND SMOTHER ME WITH KISSES??

HUH?
THE BEST DEFENSE IS A GOOD OFFENSE.

IRVING'S NEVER GOING TO SPEAK TO ME AGAIN...

NAH... IT ISN'T THAT BAD. WE'VE HAD A LITTLE SETBACK. THAT'S ALL... NOPE. THIS IS IT. THINGS DON'T GET ANY WORSE THAN THIS.

...NAH. THINGS WERE WORSE THAN THIS IN 1976. THIS IS NOTHING. JUST RIDE IT OUT AND IT WILL STABILIZE...

WHAT ARE YOU DOING, CATHY?
I'M TRYING TO DECIDE IF I'M IN A DEPRESSION OR A RECESSION.

GRANT WAS SUPPOSED TO BE HERE AT 8:00.
HE'S LATE. DUMP HIM.

DUMP HIM? MOM, IT'S ONLY 8:07.
DUMP HIM!

WAIT, MOM... HERE HE IS.
HELLO AND WELCOME TO DUMP-CITY, GRANT!!
DING DONG

HEE HEE... BLEEBLE BLEEBLE, HEE HEE...
SOMEHOW, IT'S REASSURING TO SEE WHERE MY PERSONALITY CAME FROM.

WELL?... HOW DID YOU LIKE MY MOTHER, GRANT?
CATHY, I ONLY TALKED TO HER FOR TEN SECONDS.

GRANT...
OKAY, OKAY. YOUR MOTHER IS LOVELY AND CHARMING. YOU HAVE OBVIOUSLY INHERITED ALL OF HER BEST QUALITIES...

SHE'S WARM, SENSITIVE, GRACIOUS AND BRILLIANT. A REMARKABLE WOMAN! I CERTAINLY HOPE WE CAN GET TOGETHER WITH HER AND YOUR FATHER SOON!
WHY, THANK YOU.

WHAT WAS THAT?
THE OBLIGATORY "I-JUST-MET-YOUR-MOTHER" SPEECH.

THIS IS FOR IRVING, WHO SAYS HE LOVES ME UNLESS ONE OF HIS FRIENDS IS THERE.
THIS IS FOR GRANT, WHO ACTS LIKE WE NEVER EVEN MET.
CANDY

THIS IS FOR IRVING, WHO LEAVES TOWN EVERY TIME THINGS GET SERIOUS.
THIS IS FOR GRANT, WHO SPENT THE MORNING FLIRTING WITH THE ACCOUNTING DEPARTMENT.
CANDY

THIS IS FOR IRVING, WHO SCREAMED AT ME FOR DATING GRANT.
THIS IS FOR GRANT, WHO CALLED ME A CHEAT FOR SEEING IRVING.

I'M EATING FOR TWO.
CANDY

YOU HAVE IRVING ON LINE 1, GRANT ON LINE 2, YOUR MOTHER ON LINE 3 AND AN IRATE CLIENT ON LINE 4.
RING RING RING

YOU HAVE YOUR ENTIRE LIFE FLASHING BEFORE YOUR EYES! ... WHICH ONE ARE YOU GOING TO ANSWER, CATHY???
RING RING RING

YAAA!!
CRASH

IN TIMES OF CRISIS WE FIND UNTAPPED SOURCES OF STRENGTH.

IS THIS TOO DRESSY TO WEAR TO THE OFFICE ?
YOU MUST BE KIDDING.

I'VE LOST ALL PERSPECTIVE, ANDREA.
I TOLD YOU THIS WOULD HAPPEN IF YOU STARTED DATING SOMEONE AT THE OFFICE.

CATHY, LOOK AT YOURSELF! LOOK WHAT THIS RELATIONSHIP IS DOING TO YOU !!

I THINK I LOOK PRETTY GOOD.

I CAN'T DECIDE BETWEEN THE GREEN AND THE PURPLE.

STICK WITH THE COLOR YOU WERE FIRST ATTRACTED TO, AND COORDINATION WILL BE A SNAP !

DIDN'T YOU EVER BUY SOMETHING AND THEN FIND IT PERFECTLY MATCHED SEVERAL THINGS YOU ALREADY HAD IN YOUR CLOSET ??

NO.
ME EITHER.

THE B-52's. GIVE ME A BREAK. I'M NOT GETTING UP FOR THE B-52's!
7:00

... BARRY MANILOW! YOU MUST HAVE 2 MILLION RECORDS THERE ! WHY ARE YOU PLAYING BARRY MANILOW ??!
7:45

... DISCO. HAH! I AM NOT LEAVING THIS BED UNTIL YOU PLAY A SONG I LIKE !!

IT'S THE D.J.'s FAULT.

IT'S 8:00, CATHY. AREN'T YOU GOING HOME TONIGHT?
NOT YET, CHARLENE. I HAVE SO MUCH WORK TO DO!
IN
CATHY

REPORTS TO PREPARE... NUMBERS TO GO OVER... DICTATING TO CATCH UP ON... I COULD BE HERE FOREVER!
CATH

GRANT ALREADY LEFT. HE SNEAKED OUT THE BACK DOOR TWO HOURS AGO.

GOODNIGHT, CHARLENE.
Guisewite

I ALWAYS USED TO GET MY DAD A TIE FOR HIS BIRTHDAY.
TIES

BUT NOW I'M MUCH MORE AWARE OF THE NEW "FATHERING" ROLE. THE MORE I READ ABOUT THE "SHARING AND NURTURING" FATHER...
TIE

...THE MORE I APPRECIATE THE IMPACT MY DAD HAD ON ME, AND HOW FAR AHEAD OF HIS TIME HE WAS IN THE WAY HE BROUGHT ME UP!!

SO NOW WHAT ARE YOU GOING TO GET HIM?
A TIE. BUT A MORE MEANINGFUL TIE.
TIES
Guisewite

I'M FURIOUS WITH GRANT ABOUT OUR DATE LAST NIGHT, BUT I DON'T WANT HIM TO THINK THAT'S WHY I'M CRITICIZING HIS REPORT.

I JUST HAVE TO BE DIGNIFIED, PROFESSIONAL, AND CHOOSE MY WORDS VERY CAREFULLY.

DRIVEL! DRIVEL! DRIVEL!!

...HM! IT WASN'T AS HARD AS I THOUGHT.
Guisewite

Z Z Z Z Z Z Z Z Z Z Z Z Z Z Z

YOU'RE NOT SLEEPING, ARE YOU, CATHY?
SLEEPING? OF COURSE I'M NOT SLEEPING!

YOU LOOK LIKE YOU'RE SLEEPING.
SLEEPING! DON'T BE SILLY! IT'S THE MIDDLE OF THE DAY!

IT'S HARD TO BE CONVINCING WHEN YOU HAVE YOUR NOSE STUCK IN A TYPEWRITER.
Guisewite

I THOUGHT YOU PAID BILLS ON TUESDAY NIGHT, CATHY.
NO, ANDREA. ON TUESDAY I FIND THE BILLS AND ASSEMBLE THEM INTO A NEAT STACK.

ON WEDNESDAY, I OPEN THE BILLS, GET DISGUSTED, AND GO TO THE MOVIES TO ALLEVIATE MY DEPRESSION.

ON THURSDAY, I DECIDE TO WRITE IRATE LETTERS TO ALL THE COMPANIES. FRIDAY, I ATTACK MYSELF FOR MY FINANCIAL INCOMPETENCE. AND ON SATURDAY, I ACTUALLY PAY THE BILLS.

PROPER MONEY MANAGEMENT SHOULD NEVER BE RUSHED.
Guisewite

GOOD MORNING, GRANT. WHERE'S CATHY?
SHE WAS TOO EMBARRASSED TO ARRIVE WITH ME, SO SHE'S COUNTING TO 100, AND TAKING THE NEXT ELEVATOR.

HI, CHARLENE. WHERE'S CATHY?
SHE WAS TOO EMBARRASSED TO ARRIVE WITH GRANT, SO SHE'S COUNTING TO 100, AND TAKING THE NEXT ELEVATOR.

...97... 98... 99...
BINGO!

I'M BEGINNING TO REGRET MY MEMO ON THE IMPORTANCE OF OFFICE SPIRIT.
CLAP CLAP!
CLAP CLAP CLAP!
CLAP CLAP!
CLAP CLAP
Guisewite

ANY MESSAGES, CHARLENE?
YES. THE ACCOUNTING DEPARTMENT THINKS YOU SHOULD APOLOGIZE TO GRANT, BUT PERSONNEL THINKS IT WAS ALL HIS FAULT.

MANAGEMENT IS DIVIDED: 3 ON YOUR SIDE, 3 ON GRANT'S. CLERICAL IS BEHIND YOU ALL THE WAY, EXCEPT LINDA WHO WANTS YOU AND GRANT TO BREAK UP SO SHE CAN DATE HIM.

ALSO, YOU HAD A CALL FROM A CLIENT.
THANK YOU.

HE THINKS YOU'RE BEING PETTY AND THAT YOU SHOULD INVITE GRANT OVER FOR A NICE HOT DINNER.
Guisewite

IS THIS GOING TO BE ONE OF THOSE MOTHERLY TALKS WHERE YOU CITE EXAMPLES OF WOMEN MY AGE WHO ARE DISCOVERING THE THRILL OF A FORMAL WEDDING?
NO.

OLDER WOMEN WHO REGRET NOT HAVING KIDS?
NO.
PROMISCUOUS WOMEN WHO REGRET BEING PROMISCUOUS?
NO.

DOES IT INVOLVE A DISEASE?
NOPE.
A DRUG?
NOPE.
A DEAR ABBY CLIPPING?
NOPE.

THEN WHAT?! WHAT IS IT??!
IT'S IMPORTANT FOR A MOTHER TO BUILD IN AN ELEMENT OF SUSPENSE.
Guisewite

YOU PROBABLY HAD SOME VERY GOOD REASON FOR NOT TELLING IRVING YOU WERE DATING ME, CATHY.
OF COURSE I DID, GRANT.

I WANTED TO EXPERIENCE THE THRILL OF DATING SOMEONE NEW WITHOUT JEOPARDIZING WHAT I HAD WITH HIM.

THEN IF NOTHING WORKS OUT WITH YOU I CAN GO RUNNING BACK TO IRVING WITHOUT HAVING HIM TORTURE ME ABOUT YOU FOR THE NEXT SIX MONTHS!

ISN'T IT WONDERFUL HOW YOUR PROBLEMS SOLVE THEMSELVES WHEN YOU TALK ABOUT THEM?!
Guisewite

ANYTHING TO GO OUT, CATHY ?
NO. NOTHING TO GO OUT.
OUT
IN

ANYTHING GOING OUT TODAY?
NO. NOTHING IS DONE. NOTHING IS GOING OUT.
OUT
IN

ANYTHING GOING OUT ?
NOTHING IS GOING OUT !!
OUT
IN

OUT
IN
Guisewite

NICE MOVIE, HUH, CATHY ?
WHY AREN'T WE LIKE THAT MOVIE, IRVING ?
AN OFFICER AND A GENTLEMAN

WHY AREN'T YOU LIKE THAT? WHY DON'T YOU CARRY ME OFF INTO THE SUNSET ??
NOW HOWING

WHY DO I STILL WANT TO BE CARRIED OFF INTO THE SUNSET ?? WAAH ! WHY ISN'T OUR WHOLE LIFE LIKE THAT ??!!

...NOTHING RUINS A DATE LIKE A LITTLE ROMANCE.
NOW SHOWING
Guisewite

WE WERE JUST GETTING THINGS TOGETHER, CATHY, AND NOW I HAVE TO GO TO THIS SEMINAR FOR A WEEK.
IF ONLY YOU DIDN'T HAVE TO LEAVE SO SOON.
GATE 33
PARTING
ATLANTA
8:30

WE JUST NEED MORE TIME TO FIGURE THINGS OUT...
I KNOW, GRANT. THERE'S NEVER ENOUGH TIME...

ATTENTION PASSENGERS: DUE TO BACK-UPS, THE FLIGHT TO ATLANTA WILL BE DELAYED FOUR HOURS.

FOUR HOURS ?? WHAT ARE WE SUPPOSED TO TALK ABOUT FOR FOUR HOURS ?!!
TE 33
TING
ANTA
8:30
Guisewite

WHAT ARE YOU DOING WHILE GRANT'S OUT OF TOWN?
I'M STARVING MYSELF ON A HIDEOUS DIET...

...TORTURING MYSELF WITH EXERCISES... AND ATTACKING MY FACE, HAIR, AND NAILS WITH BEAUTY TREATMENTS SO I'LL BE GORGEOUS WHEN HE GETS BACK.

CATHY, THIS IS PATHETIC. IF YOU HAD LEFT TOWN, GRANT WOULD BE USING THIS WEEK TO GO OUT WITH EVERYONE IN THE CITY.
THAT'S WHAT MAKES WOMEN SO SPECIAL, ANDREA.

...WE'RE CAPABLE OF ENTERTAINING OURSELVES.

THESE DIET BREAKFAST SQUARES ARE DISGUSTING. I SHOULD HAVE GONE ON THE CAMBRIDGE DIET TODAY... BLEAH.. THIS IS WORSE. I SHOULD HAVE GONE ON THE BEVERLY HILLS DIET...

BLEAH. I'LL NEVER STAY ON THIS. I SHOULD HAVE STARTED THE SCARSDALE DIET. NO. WAIT.. BLEAH. I'LL GO ON THE STILLMAN.. WAIT.. NO.. THE ATKINS... THE.. YEECH.. THE...
COTTAGE CHEESE

WHAT AM I DOING HERE?? FOR ONCE, WHY DON'T I JUST GO ON A SENSIBLE REDUCTION PROGRAM WHERE I RECORD EVERYTHING I EAT?!

... BREAKFAST: 13,000 CALORIES.

DIET DIARY ENTRY, THURSDAY, 9:00 A.M.: "RADICAL CHANGES IN DIET ARE TOO BIG A SHOCK TO THE SYSTEM. IT IS FAR BETTER TO SIMPLY CUT DOWN ON FATTENING FOODS."
IN
CATHY

CHOMP!
COFFEE ROOM
CLEAN-UP SCHEDULE:

CHOMP! CHOMP!
CHOMP!
CHOMP!
CHOMP!
CHOMP!

DIET DIARY ENTRY, THURSDAY, 9:06 A.M.: "CUTTING DOWN NEVER WORKS."
CATHY

I ATE A DONUT. AFTERWARDS, I REALIZED MY URGE FOR THAT DONUT WAS JUST A MANIFESTATION OF MY JOB ANXIETY.

I ATE A BOX OF COOKIES. AFTERWARDS, I REALIZED THE COOKIES WERE JUST A SYMBOLIC COMPENSATION FOR MY INABILITY TO MAINTAIN A FULFILLING RELATIONSHIP.

I ATE A CARROT. I REALIZED NOTHING.

WHY DO I ONLY GET PHILOSOPHICAL AFTER I'VE EATEN SOMETHING FATTENING ?

I HAVE 42 LETTERS TO GET OUT THIS MORNING, AND ALL I CAN THINK ABOUT IS THE DONUT I SAW ON CHARLENE'S DESK.
OUT
CATHY

I GET AS FAR AS "DEAR MR. COOPER," AND THEN THAT DONUT POPS INTO MY MIND..... GET OUT OF MY MIND, DONUT !!

I AM IN CHARGE HERE !! YOU ARE NOT GOING TO RUN MY LIFE, YOU MISERABLE LITTLE DONUT !!

"DEAR MR. COOPER, REGARDING YOUR BUDGET, WE HAVE PAID SPECIAL ATTENTION TO THE LITTLE COLORED SPRINKLES ON THE THICK FUDGE FROSTING..."

HOW'S THE DIET, CATHY?
I HAD A BLUEBERRY MUFFIN ONE INCH FROM MY MOUTH, CHARLENE... BUT I RAN INTO THE BATHROOM AND THREW IT DOWN THE TOILET !

I HAD AN UNWRAPPED CANDY BAR IN MY HANDS... I CRUSHED IT TO PIECES AND THREW IT DOWN THE TOILET !!

I WAS SECONDS AWAY FROM A CHEESE DANISH ! I SQUASHED IT WITH MY STAPLER AND THREW IT DOWN THE TOILET !!

THAT'S TERRIFIC, CATHY ! LET ME KNOW IF THERE'S ANYTHING I CAN DO.
CALL MAINTENANCE.

SO WHAT IF I EAT THIS? THIS STUPID DIET WILL NEVER WORK ANYWAY!
CATHY... IS THAT YOU? YOU LOOK GREAT!
BAKER HOURS

HI... UH.. I LOOK GREAT??
YEAH... YOU'VE REALLY LOST WEIGHT, HAVEN'T YOU?!

I LOOK LIKE I LOST WEIGHT?? YOU CAN TELL I LOST WEIGHT??
YEAH! WOW! KEEP UP THE GOOD WORK!

THERE'S NOTHING WORSE THAN GETTING A COMPLIMENT WHEN THERE'S A PIE ON ITS WAY TO YOUR STOMACH.
Guisewite

GRANT'S GOING TO BE HOME IN TWO DAYS AND I'VE ONLY LOST THREE POUNDS.
IMPATIENCE: 210 CALORIES.

I HAD A CHANCE TO BE STUNNING FOR HIS RETURN AND I THINK I BLEW IT.
INSECURITY: 550 CALORIES.

NOW I'LL NEVER MAKE IT! YAAA! TWO DAYS!! HE'LL BE HOME IN TWO DAYS!!!
ANXIETY: 9400 CALORIES.

I HAVE A FATTENING PERSONALITY.
Guisewite

OH, WHAT A BEAUTIFUL NEW DRESS, CATHY!
THERE'S NOTHING BEAUTIFUL ABOUT A MUUMUU, MOM.

I THINK IT'S JUST LOVELY!
I GAINED TEN POUNDS ON MY DIET, MOM. IT'S THE ONLY THING I COULD GET INTO.

YOU GAINED?? I THINK IT MAKES YOU LOOK VERY SLIM.
...YOU THINK SO? REALLY??... MAYBE I DON'T LOOK SO BAD...

NICE MUUMUU, CATHY. BOY, YOU MUST HAVE REALLY PIGGED OUT THIS WEEK!
NICE TRY, MOTHER.

HI, CATHY, IT'S GRANT. PINKLEY WANTS ME TO STAY AT THIS SEMINAR FOR ANOTHER WEEK.
A WEEK! I'M GETTING A WEEK'S REPRIEVE ON MY DIET!!

I WAS REALLY COUNTING ON SEEING YOU TOMORROW.
OH, THANK HEAVENS HE DOESN'T HAVE TO SEE ME THIS FAT!

I MISS YOU.
I DON'T HAVE TO SEE HIM FOR A WEEK! OH, WHAT A RELIEF! I'M SAVED!! OH, THANK YOU!!

...SO, HOW ABOUT IF YOU FLY OUT AND MEET ME FOR THE WEEKEND?
SORRY. WRONG NUMBER.
Guisewite

YOU'VE GAINED TEN POUNDS SINCE GRANT LEFT TOWN, AND THEN HE ASKED YOU TO MEET HIM IN ATLANTA THIS WEEKEND?? CATHY, WHAT DID YOU DO?!

LET'S JUST SAY I'VE LEARNED MY LESSON, ANDREA.

OH? WHAT LESSON?

YOU'RE NEVER TOO OLD TO BE BAILED OUT BY YOUR MOTHER.
Guisewite

WHY DO YOU NEED TO JOIN A HEALTH CLUB, CATHY?
I'M DESPERATE, MOM.

YOU DON'T HAVE THAT KIND OF MONEY TO THROW AROUND.
MOM, I'M DESPERATE!
PHONE

I THINK YOU LOOK WONDERFUL!
I AM DESPERATE!!

IF YOU WANT TO LOSE WEIGHT, WHY DON'T YOU JUST TRY CUTTING DOWN ON SWEETS?
I'M NOT THAT DESPERATE.
Guisewite

TWO YEARS AGO YOU BOUGHT A JUMP ROPE. YOU SAID, "IF I'VE INVESTED $5, I'LL USE IT." YOU DIDN'T.

LAST YEAR YOU BOUGHT A SWEATSUIT AND A WORKOUT ALBUM. YOU SAID, "IF I'VE INVESTED $60, I'LL USE THEM." YOU DIDN'T.

NOW YOU'RE GOING TO BUY A $500 MEMBERSHIP IN A HEALTH CLUB ?? CATHY, WHAT ARE YOU THINKING ??

THE OLDER I GET, THE MORE IT COSTS TO MAKE ME FEEL GUILTY.

OH, YES. OUR HEALTH CLUB HAS COMPLETELY SEPARATE FACILITIES FOR MEN AND WOMEN.
WONDERFUL.

SEPARATE WORK-OUT ROOMS... SEPARATE DRESSING AREAS... SEPARATE INSTRUCTORS...
WONDERFUL.

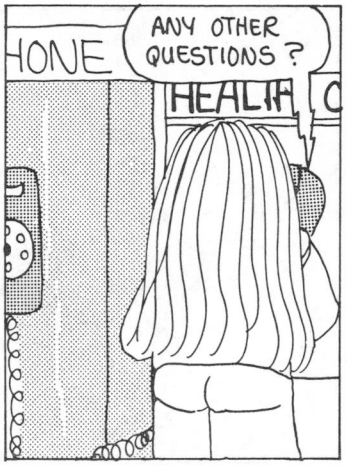
ANY OTHER QUESTIONS ?

HOW AM I SUPPOSED TO GET IN THE FRONT DOOR ?
PHONE
HEALTH CLUB

CATHY, HOW DID YOU LOSE 10 POUNDS IN 4 DAYS ??
NEW FAT IS EASIER TO LOSE THAN OLD FAT, ANDREA.

IT'S ALL TIMING. IF YOU GAIN 5 POUNDS IN ONE NIGHT, YOU COULD LOSE IT IN 2 DAYS. BUT IF YOU WAIT A WEEK, FORGET IT.

AFTER A WEEK, THE NEW FAT HAS ALREADY BECOME PART OF YOUR BODY'S FAT FAMILY AND IT'S...

... SOMETIMES I HATE THE THINGS I'M AN EXPERT ON.

I GAINED TEN POUNDS WORRYING ABOUT GRANT'S RETURN... I LOST TEN POUNDS WORRYING ABOUT GRANT'S RETURN.

TWO WEEKS OF TORTURE, AND I'M BACK TO WHERE I STARTED. FOR TWO SOLID WEEKS, I'VE AGONIZED ABOUT HOW TO LOOK AND HOW TO ACT FOR GRANT'S RETURN.

HI, CATHY. I'M BACK!
UM... HI, GRANT.

REUNIONS ARE ALWAYS A LITTLE ANTI-CLIMACTIC.
Guisewite

CANDY
MILK DUDS

CHEW CHEW
CHEW
CHEW CHEW

YES, MR. PINKLEY, I'LL DO THOSE 7 EXTRA PROJECTS! ...YES, MOM, I'LL ADDRESS 200 FLIERS FOR YOUR MEETING!... YES, ANDREA, I'D LOVE TO HELP PAINT YOUR APARTMENT!... YES, IRVING! ...YES, GRANT!... YES TO EVERYTHING!!!

NEVER GO NEAR THE PHONE WHEN YOU'RE ON A MILK DUD RUSH.
Guisewite

GRANT HAS STORMED IN THE FRONT DOOR, FOLLOWED CLOSELY BY CATHY, WHO LOOKS EQUALLY MIFFED.

CATHY HAS NOW STOMPED OUT OF HER OFFICE WITH GRANT ON HER HEELS.
RECEPTIONIST

HAS THERE BEEN A HIDEOUS FIGHT? A LOVER'S FEUD?? CATHY AND GRANT ARE...

...THIS CONCLUDES THE MORNING ANNOUNCEMENTS.
RECEPTIONIST
Guisewite

OF ALL THE NEUROTIC BEHAVIOR I'VE SEEN, GRANT, THIS TAKES THE CAKE.
GRANT

I CANNOT BELIEVE A GROWN MAN WOULD **HIDE** RATHER THAN FACE A SIMPLE RELATIONSHIP DISCUSSION!!

IRVING'S IN THE LOBBY, CATHY. HE WANTS TO KNOW WHERE YOU'VE BEEN FOR THE LAST MONTH.

MOVE OVER, GRANT.
GRANT
Guisewite

IF YOU'RE TRYING TO GET ME TO BREAK UP FIRST SO YOU WON'T HAVE IT ON YOUR CONSCIENCE, FORGET IT, GRANT. I CAN OUTLAST YOU ANY DAY!! A WOMAN CAN DRAG OUT A BREAK-UP LONGER THAN ANY MAN!!

...GET OUT OF HERE, GRANT! IT'S OVER BETWEEN US!!

HM! I USED TO HAVE MORE STAMINA THAN THAT.
Guisewite

I THOUGHT WE SHOULD INCLUDE EVERYONE. FAMILY, FRIENDS, CO-WORKERS. THEN NO ONE WOULD FEEL LEFT OUT.

BUT GRANT SAID, "NO. LET'S KEEP IT PRIVATE...TELL OUR BEST FRIENDS, AND THEN WE CAN SEND ANNOUNCEMENTS TO EVERYONE ELSE." BUT I...

CATHY, YOU MEAN YOU'RE...
BREAKING UP, MOM. WE'RE PLANNING OUR BREAK-UP.

ANOTHER DAY, ANOTHER 5000 GREY HAIRS.
Guisewite

AS YOU KNOW, CATHY AND GRANT BROKE UP THIS WEEK, CAUSING A RIPPLE EFFECT ON SEVERAL OTHER COUPLES.

JAN, WHO HAD HER EYE ON GRANT ALL ALONG, BROKE UP WITH TIM, WHO WAS SEEN...
THAT DOES IT. I AM NOT LETTING ANOTHER MEETING DETERIORATE INTO CHEAP GOSSIP!

NOW THEN, THE ECONOMIC PICTURE FOR THE REMAINDER OF THE FOURTH QUARTER HAS...

...BACK TO YOU, CHARLENE.

IT'S COLD OUT, AND IT'S GOING TO GET COLDER.

IT'S GOING TO SNOW AND HAIL AND FREEZE ALL OVER YOU.

I'M SORRY... BUT UNTIL I CAN AFFORD A HEATED GARAGE, YOU'RE JUST GOING TO HAVE TO SIT OUT HERE AND SUFFER. I'M VERY SORRY!!

WHEW! I HATE PREPARING MY CAR FOR WINTER.

HI, CHARLENE. I WAS JUST MAKING MORE COFFEE.
I DON'T HAVE TIME TO WAIT... I'LL JUST STICK MY CUP UNDER THERE.

I'M LATE FOR A MEETING. LET ME GET MY CUP IN THERE AFTER YOURS, CHARLENE.

I'M RIGHT BEHIND YOU, MR. PINKLEY. WE'LL SWITCH ON "THREE". ONE... TWO...

SOMETIMES TEAMWORK WORKS FOR YOU, SOMETIMES IT DOESN'T.

WHY SHOULD I SPEND $500 ON THIS HEALTH CLUB WHEN I CAN GO JOGGING FOR FREE?
THE HEALTH CLUB PROVIDES A FAR MORE COMPLETE EXERCISE PROGRAM.
HEALTH CLUB & FITNESS CENTER
NEW MEMBERS

NAH...
THE HEALTH CLUB AMBIANCE IS A POWERFUL PSYCHOLOGICAL MOTIVATOR TO KEEP YOU WORKING TOWARDS YOUR GOALS.

NAH...
THE HEALTH CLUB IS A CENTER FOR INTELLIGENT, SUCCESSFUL, GORGEOUS, MUSCLE-Y MEN.

BINGO.
SIGN RIGHT HERE.
GUISEWITE

NOW THEN... YOU SAID, "THE HEALTH CLUB IS A CENTER FOR INTELLIGENT, SUCCESSFUL, GORGEOUS, MUSCLE-Y MEN."
CORRECT.

BY THAT DID YOU MEAN INTELLIGENT MEN, SUCCESSFUL MEN, GORGEOUS MEN, AND MUSCLE-Y MEN? FOUR DIFFERENT TYPES OF MEN?
HEALTH CLUB & FITNESS CENTER
NEW MEMBER

OR DID YOU MEAN THE CLUB IS A CENTER FOR MEN WHO HAVE ALL FOUR OF THESE QUALITIES IN ONE?? OR DID YOU MEAN THAT SOME OF THE MEN HAVE SOME OF THESE QUALITIES??

I NEVER SIGN A CONTRACT UNTIL I UNDERSTAND ALL THE FACTS.
GUISEWITE

THERE'S JUST A TOUCH OF STUFFING LEFT. WHO WILL CLEAN IT UP SO WE CAN STACK THESE PLATTERS?

IF SOMEONE WOULD EAT THAT LAST BLOB OF POTATOES, WE WOULDN'T HAVE TO DIRTY UP ANOTHER FOOD STORAGE CONTAINER.

LOOK AT THIS PIE. WHO'LL HAVE ANOTHER SLIVER SO WE CAN EVEN OFF THE PIE?

WE'RE FAT, BUT WE'RE NEAT.
GUISEWITE

AS PART OF OUR HEALTH CLUB PROGRAM, EACH NEW MEMBER GETS A FREE INTRODUCTORY ANALYSIS.

NOW THEN, WHAT ARE YOUR PROBLEM AREAS?
NONE OF YOUR BUSINESS.
WHAT ARE YOUR FITNESS GOALS?
THAT'S PRIVATE.
DO YOU HOPE TO GAIN OR LOSE WEIGHT?
HAH!

I SEE. WELL, LET'S JUST TAKE A FEW...
DON'T COME NEAR ME WITH THAT TAPE MEASURER, YOU TOOTHPICK!!

WHAT DID YOU LEARN IN YOUR ANALYSIS, CATHY?
NEVER GO TO THE HEALTH CLUB THE DAY AFTER THANKSGIVING.
Guisewite

THE SECOND I TELL MYSELF I CAN'T HAVE ANY CAKE, I GET OBSESSED WITH HAVING SOME. IT'S RIDICULOUS.

I'LL BET IF SOMEONE PUT A CAKE IN FRONT OF ME AND TOLD ME TO EAT IT, I WOULDN'T EVEN WANT IT.

WOULD YOU LIKE A PIECE OF CAKE, CATHY?
YES!

NEVER TRUST A DIETING MIND.
Guisewite

CATHY, DIDN'T YOU DO ANYTHING DURING THE 6 WEEKS YOU WERE SEEING GRANT??
NO.

I'M 6 WEEKS BEHIND ON WORK, BILLS, LAUNDRY, CLEANING... I'VE LOST TOUCH WITH MY PARENTS AND MY FRIENDS.

IT'S ACTUALLY A RELIEF TO HAVE THAT RELATIONSHIP OVER WITH SO I CAN GET BACK TO MY NORMAL LIFE.

...IRVING!!
YOU'VE HAD 6 WEEKS TO YOURSELF, SWEETIE.. ..YOU'D BETTER BE READY TO SPEND SOME TIME WITH ME!
Guisewite

WHAT HAVE YOU BEEN DOING FOR THE LAST SIX WEEKS, CATHY ?
THAT DEPENDS, IRVING.

IF I TOLD YOU I'D BEEN SEEING SOMEONE ELSE WOULD YOU BE REPULSED AND STORM OFF ?... OR WOULD YOU RESPECT AND LOVE ME FOR MY HONESTY ?

...OR WOULD YOU FIND ME EVEN MORE APPEALING SINCE ANOTHER MAN HAD BEEN ATTRACTED TO ME ??

I HATE IT WHEN HE MAKES ME GUESS.
Guisewite

HURRY, CHARLENE ! I HAVE TO GET THESE OUT SO I CAN GET TO MY AEROBICS CLASS BY 6:00 !

YAAA ! IT'S 5:45 ! HURRY HURRY, HURRY !
SCRAPE!
CHIP!
SCRAPE

5:58... 5:59... WAIT ! I'M COMING ! WAIT FOR ME !!
HEALTH CLUB

OKAY, CLASS... LET'S GET READY TO MOVE !!
Guisewite

PLEASE, CATHY ! IT'S AN EMERGENCY !!
EVERY SCRAP OF PAPER THAT'S COME THROUGH THIS OFFICE IN THE LAST 5 YEARS HAS BEEN AN EMERGENCY.

IN THE BIG PICTURE OF LIFE WHAT DIFFERENCE WILL THIS ONE MEASLY PROJECT OUT OF OUR PUNY OFFICE MAKE ??

WHO CARES IF THE STUPID CLIENT GETS HIS STUPID FIGURES ?!
YOU CAN'T GET IT DONE BY MONDAY?

DON'T BE RIDICULOUS. I WON'T EVEN BE FINISHED COMPLAINING ABOUT IT BY THEN.
Guisewite

SOMEHOW FRANK ALWAYS KNOWS WHEN I NEED A LITTLE GIFT TO PICK ME UP.
SOMEHOW BOB ALWAYS KNOWS WHEN I NEED A KISS.

SOMEHOW MARK ALWAYS KNOWS WHEN I NEED TIME TO MYSELF.
SOMEHOW PAUL ALWAYS KNOWS WHEN I NEED WINE AND ROSES.
DING DONG

SOMEHOW IRVING ALWAYS KNOWS WHEN MY HAIR IS FILTHY.

YOU DIDN'T JOG IN THE 70's? EVERYONE JOGGED IN THE 70's!
NO. NO, I NEVER JOGGED.
HEALTH CLUB

WELL, YOU WENT BIKE RIDING IN THE 60's, DIDN'T YOU? EVERYONE GOT A 10-SPEED IN THE 60's.
NO, UM... I NEVER BOUGHT A BIKE.

YOU'VE MISSED TWO ENTIRE DECADES OF AMERICAN FITNESS. I CAN'T BELIEVE IT!!
ME EITHER.

I'M GOING TO BE THE ONLY FAT GRANDMOTHER IN THE 21st CENTURY.

TA DA!!
YOU FINISHED THE DRAPE PROJECT?? CONGRATULATIONS, CATHY!!!

THANK YOU, MR. PINKLEY. OH, WHAT A RELIEF! OH, IT'S FINALLY FINISHED!!!
IT'S FINISHED! I WONDER IF YOU...

ANYTHING, MR. PINKLEY! AFTER THAT ONE, I'M READY FOR ANYTHING!!

NOTHING SETS ME BACK LIKE A BIG VICTORY.

$89.88! THEY WANT $89.88 FOR THIS!
$89.88! YAAA!!
HOLIDAY BLOUSES

$73.40! YAAA!
$73.40?! I SAW THAT FOR $68.00 AT THE MALL!!
Special

$199.00! WHO COULD PAY $199.00?!
YAAA! THOSE USED TO COST $15.00!!
BRIEFCASE

MAY I HELP YOU?
NO. WE'RE JUST COMPARISON SCREAMING.
Guisewite

HI THERE, SWEETIE. IT'S ME. I WAS JUST THINKING ABOUT YOU AND, UH, I THOUGHT I'D SAY HELLO.

SO, UM... HA, HA... HELLO! OH, HEE, HEE, HEE... AHEM.. THIS IS STUPID.

NO, REALLY, I WAS JUST SITTING HERE AND HEE HEE HA, HA! HOO HA! WAIT... I'M.. AHEM.. HOO HA HA HA!!

EXCUSE ME, MOM. I HAVE TO GO BREAK INTO IRVING'S APARTMENT AND RIP THE TAPE OUT OF HIS PHONE ANSWERING MACHINE.
Guisewite

"MANY BUSY CAREER WOMEN DO THEIR CHRISTMAS SHOPPING BY CATALOG, IN THE RELAXING ATMOSPHERE OF THEIR OWN HOMES."

I THOUGHT WE HAD A DATE TONIGHT, CATHY!
YOUR BATHTUB OVERFLOWED AND MADE MY CEILING LEAK!!
WHAT'S HE DOING HERE?!

WHERE'S YOUR RENT??
WHERE'S MY BOYFRIEND?!
WHERE'S MY TIE?!
WHERE'S DINNER?!
WHERE'S YOUR PHONE BILL?!
WHERE'S THE ARGUS PROJECT?!

...MANY BUSY CAREER WOMEN FIND A MOBBED DEPARTMENT STORE MORE RELAXING.
Guisewite

THIS WOULD BE PERFECT FOR IRVING...
OH, NO. IT TAKES 4 WEEKS TO DELIVER.
CHRISTMAS CATALOGS
CATALOGS

MOM WOULD LOVE THIS...
NOPE. 6 WEEK DELIVERY.
THIS WOULD BE WONDER-FUL FOR...
NOPE. 3 WEEKS TO ENGRAVE, 3 TO DELIVER.

I'LL TAKE ANYTHING! I'LL TAKE ANYTHING YOU CAN GET TO ME BEFORE CHRISTMAS!!
CATALOGS
CATALOGS

HOW'S YOUR SHOPPING GOING?
NOT BAD. I'M USUALLY NOT THIS PANICKED FOR ANOTHER 2 WEEKS.
Groening

HI. HOW DO YOU LIKE THE HEALTH CLUB?
I LOVE IT. THIS CLUB IS GIVING ME A WHOLE NEW PERSPECTIVE ON MYSELF!

I'M GOING TO MAKE THIS CLUB A REGULAR PART OF EVERY DAY FOR THE REST OF MY LIFE!!!

I LOVE IT, TOO. I'VE BEEN COMING HERE FOR TWO YEARS!

I QUIT.
Groening

AT FIRST, IT ALL LOOKS SO APPEALING. YOU WANT IT ALL.
HOLIDAY SPECIAL
SALE

THEN YOU LOOK A LITTLE CLOSER. EH... THAT'S NOT QUITE RIGHT. NAH... THAT WON'T QUITE DO IT.
CHRISTMAS GIFTS
SOAP

PRETTY SOON YOU REALIZE THAT OF THE 42 BILLION ITEMS OFFERED, THERE'S NOT ONE THING THAT'S EXACTLY WHAT YOU WANT.

SHOPPING IS A LOT LIKE DATING.
HOLIDAY HOURS 9-9:00
Groening

WE HAVE CALCULATOR CHECK-BOOKS, CALCULATOR WATCHES, CALCULATOR CREDIT CARD CASES, CALCULATOR LAMPS...

CALCULATOR PICTURE FRAMES, CALCULATOR PENS, CALCULATOR ATTACHÉ CASES, CALCULATOR LIGHTERS, CALCULATOR RINGS, CALCULATOR PHONES...

THIS YEAR WHY NOT GIVE THE GIFT OF A CALCULATOR TO EVERYONE ON YOUR LIST?

NOBODY I KNOW HAS ANYTHING TO ADD UP.
Guisewite

MM...THIS WOULD MAKE A NICE GIFT..NO, MAYBE THIS ONE...NOW I CAN'T TELL WHICH IS WHICH...WAIT.. HERE'S A BLANK SPACE ON MY ARM... OOH, HERE'S A NEW ONE...
COLOGNE DEPT.
SQUIRT
SQUIRT
SQUIRT
SQUIRT

CATHY, HOW COULD YOU TAKE A 2-HOUR LUNCH WHEN WE HAVE...

Thunk!

THE PROPER COLOGNE CAN CHANGE YOUR WHOLE LIFE.
Guisewite

HOW ABOUT THIS NICE...
NO. IRVING HATES MECHANICAL THINGS.
Christmas Cameras
SALE
CAMERA

HOW ABOUT...
NO. HE HATES TIES. HE HATES SWEATERS. HE HATES ALL SHIRTS PICKED OUT BY WOMEN.
GIFTS

HOW ABOUT...
NOPE. HE HATES VINYL, VELOUR, JEWELRY, GREEN, AND EVERY-THING ELECTRICAL.
FOR HIM

I KNOW YOU TOO WELL TO BUY YOU A PRESENT.
Guisewite

TO THE ANDREWS FAMILY... WISHING YOU A WARM AND WONDERFUL CHRISTMAS. I HOPE 1983 WILL BE A SPECIAL YEAR FULL OF LOVE AND PROSPERITY.

TO THE BURKOFF FAMILY... BEST WISHES FOR A VERY MERRY CHRISTMAS AND THE HAPPIEST OF NEW YEARS.

DEAR DIGGS FAMILY... MERRY CHRISTMAS, HAPPY NEW YEAR.
DEAR SALEMS... MERRY CHRISTMAS.
DEAR WILSONS... GREETINGS.

PEOPLE TOWARD THE END OF THE ALPHABET DON'T GET MUCH IN THE WAY OF CHRISTMAS NOTES.
Guisewite

BUY ONE OF THESE NEW POUFFY TAFFETA DRESSES AND YOU'LL BE THE CENTER OF ATTENTION AT ALL YOUR HOLIDAY FUNCTIONS!

I SEE WHAT YOU MEAN.

THERE WILL ONLY BE ROOM FOR ONE OTHER PERSON AT EVERY PARTY.
Guisewite

OKAY. I LIED. I DIDN'T GO OUT OF TOWN.

I WAS AFRAID YOU'D YELL AT ME IF I JUST TOLD YOU I WAS TOO BUSY.

LOOK, LOTS OF THINGS ARE IMPORTANT TO ME. I PROMISE TO FIND MORE TIME IN THE FUTURE, BUT NOT THE WEEK BEFORE CHRISTMAS!
CARDS

BRAVO, CATHY! WHAT DID IRVING SAY??
THAT WASN'T IRVING. IT WAS MY AEROBICS TEACHER.
Guisewite

WHERE DID YOU BUY THIS, MOM? THIS WOULD BE PERFECT FOR ANDREA.
TAKE IT, CATHY. I HADN'T DECIDED WHO TO GIVE IT TO.

ARE YOU SURE?... WOAH! THIS WOULD BE GREAT FOR THE DALES!
TAKE IT, SWEETIE. I CAN GET ANOTHER ONE.
TAPE

REALLY?...OOH! WHAT'S THIS?
TAKE IT!
IRVING WOULD LOVE THIS!
TAKE IT!
THIS IS GORGEOUS!
TAKE IT!

A MOTHER'S SHOPPING IS NEVER DONE.
Guisewite

HEE, HEE... THE MORTON TWINS HAVE TURNED INTO REGULAR LITTLE BLIMPS.
MOM, THAT'S TERRIBLE!
Christmas Cards

...HEE, HEE.. MR. FRAME HAS SEVEN CHINS!
CATHY, THAT'S TERRIBLE!
Christmas Cards

...HEE, HEE.. WHAT HAPPENED TO MARTHA'S HAIR??!
HEE, HEE, HEE! OH, WHAT FUN!
Christmas Cards
Guisewite

WHY DON'T WE EVER SEND OUT PHOTO CHRISTMAS CARDS?
Christmas Cards

I'D BETTER TASTE THE DOUGH. I CAN'T TELL IF IT'S RIGHT UNLESS I TASTE IT.
MILK
CHRISTMAS COOKIES

NOW I HAVE TO TASTE A PARTIALLY DONE COOKIE TO MAKE SURE THE BATCH IS BAKING PROPERLY.
FLOUR

NOW I MUST TASTE THE COOLED COOKIES TO MAKE SURE THEY AREN'T OVER OR UNDER-COOKED!!
SUGAR

PERFECTIONISTS TEND TO BE OVERWEIGHT.
Guisewite

A PRACTICAL GIFT TELLS HIM THE ROMANCE IS OVER. A PERSONAL GIFT TELLS HIM THE ROMANCE HAS JUST BEGUN.

AN INTIMATE GIFT SAYS YOU WANT TO GET CLOSER. A KITCHEN GIFT SAYS YOU WANT HIM TO CHANGE. A SPORTS GIFT SAYS YOU WANT HIM TO THINK YOU UNDERSTAND HIM.

A HAND-MADE GIFT SAYS, "I'M SWEET AND HOMEY"... AN EXPENSIVE GIFT SAYS, "I'M INDEPENDENT AND WORLDLY AND AWARE!!"

WHAT DID YOU DECIDE TO GET IRVING?
THE GIFT OF CONFUSION.

AS EACH GIFT IS OPENED, FATHER WILL NEATLY FOLD THE GIFT WRAP FOR RE-USE, AND I WILL RECORD WHO EACH PRESENT IS FROM SO WE'LL HAVE A COMPLETE LIST FOR OUR THANK YOU NOTES!
Merry Christmas

...NOT BAD. AT LEAST THIS YEAR I HAD TIME TO GET MY WHOLE SPEECH OUT.

MORE PIE?
MORE COOKIES?
MORE STRUDEL?
MORE NUT BREAD?
MORE CANDY?

THERE ARE DEEP, PSYCHOLOGICAL REASONS FOR WHY MOTHERS STUFF THEIR CHILDREN WITH FOOD OVER THE HOLIDAYS, MOM.
I KNOW, CATHY.

IF I FATTEN YOU UP, YOU'LL BE TOO EMBARRASSED TO LEAVE THE HOUSE, SO YOU'LL STAY LONGER!

...SO MUCH FOR INTROSPECTION.

I WISH YOU DIDN'T HAVE TO GO RUSHING OFF TO SEE IRVING, SWEETIE.
YOU'RE RUSHING OFF?
I'M NOT RUSHING OFF.

IF IRVING'S SO WONDERFUL, WHERE WAS HE WHEN YOU HAD MEASLES IN THE 1st GRADE?
I THOUGHT YOU BROKE UP WITH IRVING.

YOU'RE LEAVING THE PARENTS WHO LOVE YOU TO EXCHANGE GIFTS WITH A MAN YOU BROKE UP WITH ??
DOES IRVING HAVE A JOB YET? DOES IRVING HAVE A FUTURE ??

...I KNOW, SWEETIE! WHY DON'T YOU JUST HAVE IRVING COME OVER HERE?!
Guisewite

CLICK! CLICK!
THE SUITCASE IS COMING OUT. CATHY'S GETTING READY TO LEAVE.

YAAACK! THE SUITCASE IS OUT! THE SUITCASE IS OUT!!!

I HATE YOU, YOU STUPID SUITCASE!!

...AND MOTHERS WONDER WHY WE WAIT UNTIL THE LAST SECOND TO PACK.
Guisewite

DO YOU THINK CATHY HAD A GOOD TIME WITH US OVER CHRISTMAS?
WHY? JUST BECAUSE YOU ASKED ABOUT HER LOVE LIFE EVERY TEN MINUTES?

HOW ABOUT WHEN I TOLD HER TO RINSE HER DIRTY DISHES OR THERE'D BE NO DESSERT? THAT REALLY BUGGED HER!
HA, HA! THEN I GAVE HER MY ANNUAL INVESTMENT LECTURE! SHE HATES THAT!

HOO, HA! DID YOU SEE HER FACE WHEN I WHIPPED OUT MY CARTON OF CLIPPINGS?!
HOO, BOY! THEN THE CAR DISCUSSION... THEN THE HAIR DISCUSSION... WHAT A VISIT!!

NOT MANY FAMILIES COULD PACK SO MUCH INTO SIX SHORT DAYS.
Guisewite

...AND LASTLY, I WILL NEVER AGAIN THROW DRIED-OUT PENS BACK IN MY DESK DRAWER!
SUGAR

GOOD FOR YOU, CATHY.

BY MAKING A SMALL NEW YEAR'S RESOLUTION THAT YOU **KNOW** YOU CAN KEEP, YOU'LL GAIN THE CONFIDENCE YOU NEED TO STICK TO YOUR BIG RESOLUTION!!

THAT **WAS** MY BIG RESOLUTION.
GUISEWITE

I REMEMBER THAT SONG! THAT WAS #1 THE DAY I OVERSLEPT AND RAN INTO THE DRAPE MEETING WITH HOT ROLLERS IN MY HAIR!

OH, AND THAT ONE...THAT WAS #1 THE DAY I GOT STUCK IN TRAFFIC, CAUSING 16 SERVINGS OF "LASAGNA FOR ONE" TO THAW PREMATURELY IN MY TRUNK!

OH, WAIT! HERE'S MY FAVORITE! THIS SONG HIT #1 THE DAY THAT EVERY MECHANICAL, ELECTRICAL AND DIGITAL THING I OWN BLEW UP WITHIN TEN MINUTES OF EACH OTHER!!

I CAN'T BELIEVE THIS, CATHY.
I KNOW. 1982'S GOING TO BE HARD TO TOP.
GUISEWITE

ARE YOU STILL ADMIRING THAT THING?
THERE'S NOTHING IN THE WORLD LIKE A NEW CALENDAR, CHARLENE.

THINK OF THE HISTORY THAT WILL UNFOLD ON THESE PAGES! I WILL RECORD EVERY ACCOMPLISHMENT! EVERY TRIUMPH!!
1983

CATHY, IT'S 10:45!!

"MONDAY, JAN. 3, 1983: MISSED THE STYLECRAFT MEETING BY TWO HOURS."
GUISEWITE

FIND OUT WHAT YOU DID AT THE OFFICE HOLIDAY PARTY
PRICES: $5 AND UP

DO YOU ACTUALLY EXPECT ME TO PAY $5 TO READ GOSSIP ABOUT MYSELF, CHARLENE?
NO. BUT I THOUGHT YOU'D PAY $15 TO READ ABOUT PINKLEY, OR $25 FOR GRANT.

IN FACT, I THOUGHT YOU MIGHT EVEN GO THE FULL $89.95 FOR THE COMPLETE BOUND SET: "THE 1982 OFFICE PARTY IN REVIEW"!

A SMART RETAILER KNOWS HER CUSTOMERS.
FIND OUT WHAT YOU DID AT THE OFFICE HOLIDAY PAR
PRICES: $5 AND

IF I BUY A PIE AT THE 7-11 AT MIDNIGHT ON JANUARY 5th, EVERYONE WILL KNOW I'M CHEATING ON MY NEW YEAR'S DIET.

SO WHAT? WHAT DO I CARE IF THE CASHIER AT THE 7-11 THINKS I'M CHEATING ON MY DIET?? HAH!

HELLO I WOULD LIKE TO BUY THIS PIE AND I DON'T CARE WHAT YOU THINK!!!

WHAT'S HAPPENED TO YOUR DIET, CATHY?
MY STRONG SIDE KEEPS SHOWING UP AT THE WRONG TIME.

WHY ARE YOU MAKING SUCH A BIG DEAL ABOUT RETURNING THE MAKE-UP BAG YOU GOT FOR ANDREA?
SOME SALESPERSON WAS COUNTING ON THE COMMISSION FROM THIS, MOM.

OH, FOR HEAVEN'S SAKE, CATHY. EVERYONE RETURNS THINGS AFTER CHRISTMAS.
HI. I'D LIKE TO RETURN THIS.

CALL EDITH AND TELL HER TO CUT THE VACATION SHORT! HER MAKE-UP BAG SALE JUST FELL THROUGH!!

HAPPY MOTHER'S DAY, MOM.
YOU SHOULDN'T HAVE.

HAVE WE RECUPERATED FROM THE HOLIDAYS YET, CATHY ?
WELL, LET'S SEE... TODAY BRIAN ACCUSED FRANK OF STEALING HIS ACCOUNT...

MARK ACCUSED JACK OF STEALING HIS GIRLFRIEND... PAM ACCUSED JOE OF STEALING HER CELERY... AND CHARLENE SPENT THE MORNING SCREAMING AT EVERYONE FOR REFUSING TO ATTEND THE NEW COPIER DEMONSTRATION.
SUGAR

OUT OF A COMPANY OF 45 PEOPLE, ONLY 3 ARE ACTUALLY SPEAKING TO EACH OTHER.

AT LAST ! THINGS ARE FINALLY BACK TO NORMAL!
Guisewite

IRVING'S BEEN GONE FOR A WEEK AND HE HASN'T CALLED ONCE.
THEN THIS IS PROBABLY HIM.
RING RING!

WHAT DO I SAY ? SHOULD I ACT MAD ? SHOULD I LET HIM KNOW I'M HURT ?
RING RING!

SWEETIE, JUST PICK UP THE PHONE AND SAY THOSE THREE MAGIC LITTLE WORDS.
RING RING!

IS SHE SKINNY ?!
Guisewite

EARLIER TODAY YOU TURNED DOWN A 15¢ DONUT, A 35¢ COOKIE, AND A 50¢ CUPCAKE...

... AND NOW YOU'RE DIVING INTO A $10.00 BOX OF GOURMET CHOCOLATES.

CATHY, HOW COULD YOU DO THIS TO YOURSELF ??!

I WAS HOPING THE MORE EXPENSIVE FAT WOULD LOOK BETTER ON ME.
Guisewite

WE HAVE THE AUTO-REDIAL TELEPHONE WITH 9, 15, OR 32-NUMBER MEMORY... THE ALL-ELECTRONIC MINI-PHONE... CORDLESS, COLLAPSIBLE OR CALCULATOR PHONES...

PHONES WITH A MUTE SWITCH, RINGER ON/OFF SWITCH, AND/OR AMPLIFIER SWITCH. PHONES THAT WILL ANSWER, RECORD, TIME CALLS OR TURN ELECTRICAL APPLIANCES ON OR OFF FROM ANYWHERE IN THE WORLD!

DO YOU HAVE ANY PHONES THAT WILL NOT RING SO MUCH AT THE OFFICE, BUT WILL RING MORE AT HOME?
NO.

ONCE AGAIN, MODERN TECHNOLOGY ZOOMS PAST THE OBVIOUS.
PHONE CENTER
GUISEWITE

WHAT HAPPENED HERE?!
I STUFFED MY PHONE BILL DOWN THE GARBAGE DISPOSAL AND IT BROKE.

JOE PLUMBING

THAT WILL BE $42.00.
$42.00?? BLAAAA!!
RIP!!

APARTMENT 365: HOME OF THE DAILY COMPOUNDED DEBT.
JOE PLUMBING
GUISEWITE

YOU SEEM TO INTUITIVELY KNOW HOW TO HANDLE THE OZWELL CLIENT, CATHY. PLEASE CALL AND EXPLAIN WHY WE'RE $12,000.00 OVER BUDGET.

I HAVE ALWAYS FOUGHT FOR WOMEN'S RIGHTS. WANT TO COME OVER AND SEE MY FILE OF CORRESPONDENCE WITH PRO-WOMAN LEGISLATORS??

I LOVE AND RESPECT YOU ENOUGH TO KNOW YOU NEED TIME TO YOURSELF, MY DARLING. BYE.

MEN ARE REALLY STARTING TO CHANGE, AREN'T THEY?
YES. THEY'RE GETTING SNEAKIER.
MEN IN THE 80'S
GUISEWITE

THIS SHOWER CURTAIN IS DISGUSTING. THE SECOND I GET HOME FROM WORK, I'M GOING TO DISINFECT THIS SHOWER CURTAIN!

THIS CLOSET IS DISGUSTING. THE SECOND I GET HOME FROM WORK, I'M GOING TO ORGANIZE THIS CLOSET!

THIS CAR IS DISGUSTING. THE SECOND I GET HOME FROM WORK, I'M GOING TO CLEAN OUT THIS CAR!!

PLEASE MAKE ME WORK LATE TONIGHT, MR. PINKLEY.
Gruisewitz

ONE FOR DINNER.
DINING ALONE, MISS? HOW ABOUT THIS PUNY TABLE NEXT TO THE KITCHEN?

MAY I HAVE A MENU, PLEASE?
HEY SAM! THE LADY WITH NO DATE WANTS A MENU!!

CHECK! I'VE BEEN WAITING 45 MINUTES FOR MY CHECK!!
WHAT'S THE MATTER? AFRAID YOU'RE GOING TO MISS OUT ON SOME SHOPPING TIME??

...ISN'T THAT JUST LIKE A WOMAN TO NOT LEAVE A DECENT TIP??
Gruisewitz

...SO THE SHIPMENT DIDN'T COME, LEAVING ME WITH...
IRVING, HONEY, TONIGHT IS MY "COMPLAINT NIGHT," REMEMBER?

WHAT ARE YOU TALKING ABOUT? YOU BEEFED ABOUT YOUR JOB FOR TWO HOURS LAST NIGHT.
I WAS JUST SHOWING COMPASSION FOR YOUR COMPLAINT. LAST NIGHT WAS YOURS.

TONIGHT WE SHARE IN MY PROBLEMS!!!

I DON'T KNOW HOW MANY MORE YEARS OF THE "US DECADE" I CAN TAKE.
Gruisewitz

I'M GOING TO HAVE TO WORK LATE TOMORROW, IRVING.
FINE. YOU'RE INDEPENDENT. YOU DON'T NEED ME. WHO CARES?

I'M NOT WORKING LATE TONIGHT, SWEETIE...
AAACK! TOO CLINGY! TOO DEMANDING! YOU'RE SUFFOCATING ME!!

I MAY OR MAY NOT BE FREE ON THURSDAY.
VAGUE AND INDECISIVE, AS USUAL.

WHY CAN'T WOMEN EVER FIGURE OUT WHAT THEY WANT IN A RELATIONSHIP??

UH, OH. I FORGOT WHERE I'M SUPPOSED TO PICK UP MY EXERCISE CARD.
HEALTH CLUB
Aerobics Classes

I FORGOT WHERE THE WOMEN'S LOCKER ROOM IS. I FORGOT TO BRING A LOCK, SO I CAN'T CHANGE MY CLOTHES ANYWAY.
MEN

I FORGOT WHICH MACHINES I'M SUPPOSED TO USE. I FORGOT WHAT TO DO ON THE ONES I DO USE...

...MANY OF OUR MEMBERS ENJOY COMING HERE RIGHT FROM THE OFFICE.
TOURS

YOU'VE BEEN AVOIDING ME, IRVING. I CAN ONLY ASSUME YOU MET SOMEONE NEW AND ARE AFRAID TO TELL ME.

OR I COULD ASSUME YOUR TRIP GAVE YOU A NEW PERSPECTIVE AND YOU'RE SICK OF THIS RELATIONSHIP.
BREAD

OR, I COULD ASSUME YOU'RE MADLY IN LOVE WITH ME AND YOU'RE JUST ACTING BLASÉ AS A FINAL, DESPERATE MOVE TO ENTICE ME!!

WAIT A MINUTE. I...
TOO LATE. I ALREADY MADE MY CHOICE.

WHERE DID YOU GET THIS GORGEOUS TEA SET, IRVING?
MY MOTHER.

YOUR MOTHER. HAH. THIS IS A GIFT FROM ANOTHER WOMAN!

THIS IS A GIFT FROM A RICH, REDHEADED WOMAN WHO COOKED YOU JAPANESE FOOD BY CANDLELIGHT IN HER OAK AND CHROME CONDOMINIUM AND THEN BOUGHT YOU THIS AS A MEMENTO OF THE EVENING!

THANK HEAVENS SHE DIDN'T GET ME A BATHROBE.
GUISEWITE

CATHY'S MAD AT ME. I SHOULD CALL HER AND APOLOGISE.

BUT THEN WHAT? SHE'LL THINK WE'RE BACK TOGETHER. ...MAYBE SHE WON'T SPEAK TO ME. I'LL HAVE TO BEG HER TO GET BACK TOGETHER.

WHY SHOULD I BEG HER TO GET BACK TOGETHER IF I DON'T EVEN KNOW IF I WANT TO GET BACK TOGETHER??!

THIS IS WHY GOD INVENTED FOOTBALL.
CLICK!
GUISEWITE

I CARE FOR YOU, CATHY, BUT I'M JUST NOT READY FOR A BIG COMMITMENT.

MAYBE SOMEDAY...BUT FOR NOW I NEED TIME TO MYSELF TO WORK OUT WHO I AM AND WHAT I WANT.

I HOPE WE CAN STILL BE FRIENDS, OR AT LEAST THAT YOU'LL ONE DAY REMEMBER ME WITH THE FONDNESS THAT I'LL ALWAYS REMEMBER YOU.

THE REAL CLASSICS ARE NEVER FORGOTTEN.
GUISEWITE

I DON'T MIND EATING OUT ALONE...I SORT OF LIKE EATING OUT ALONE.

I AM PROUD TO BE EATING OUT ALONE!!

ONE FETTUCINI ALFREDO WITH A PLATTER OF SPAGHETTI ON THE SIDE!

MY DATE WILL BE ALONG SHORTLY.
GUISEWITE

HERE, CATHY.
OH, NOT THERE. INCOMING MAIL GOES IN MY "TO BE WRITTEN TO IMMEDIATELY" STACK.

A MONTH LATER, I MOVE IT TO MY "TO BE CALLED IMMEDIATELY" STACK. A WEEK AFTER THAT, IT GOES BACK IN THE "TO BE WRITTEN TO" STACK. THEN BACK TO "TO BE CALLED"...

AFTER 6 REVOLUTIONS, I CRAM IT INTO MY FILE AND PRETEND IT NEVER ARRIVED.

WHY DON'T YOU JUST THROW IT OUT WHEN IT COMES AND SAVE YOURSELF THE HASSLE?
SOME PEOPLE HAVE NO RESPECT FOR THE ROUTING SYSTEM.
GUISEWITE

YVONNE BROUGHT THE HOMEMADE SPINACH PASTA, SEASONED WITH HERBS FROM HER WINDOWSILL HERB GARDEN.

RAYMOND HAND-GROUND THE FLOUR FOR HIS LOVELY ALMOND-FIG LOAF, SERVED WITH KIM'S INCOMPARABLE PLUM PRESERVES!

THE KLEINS BROUGHT THE SPECTACULAR BLANCHED CRUDITE PLATTER, HOME-GROWN SPROUTS, WITH A DIP OF HOMEMADE YOGURT AND HONEY GATHERED FROM THEIR OWN HIVE!

CATHY IS THE ONE WHO JUST LEFT WITH THE MARSHMALLOW JELLO MOLD IN HER PURSE.
GUISEWITE

I KNOW WHERE EVERY LADIES' ROOM IN THE CITY IS.

I CAN LOOK AT A RACK OF 700 KINDS OF PANTYHOSE AND MAKE MY SELECTION IN TWO SECONDS FLAT!

I KNOW SIX WAYS TO RE-HEM A SKIRT WITHOUT THREAD... ..AND WITH THE ENTIRE WORLD CRASHING AROUND ME, I'M ABLE TO FOCUS ON ONE SPLIT-END FOR UP TO AN HOUR!!!

HOW'S THE RESUME COMING?
NOT BAD. SO FAR, I'M "INFORMED, DECISIVE, RESOURCEFUL AND DILIGENT."
Guisewite

SO, UM.. HOW LONG HAVE YOU BEEN IN THE COMMODITIES FIELD?
WELL, I...
ONE ORDER OF POTATO SKINS SMOTHERED WITH BACON BITS, CHEESE AND SOUR CREAM...

I WANT TO GO HOME NOW.
ME TOO.

FIRST DATES LASTED LONGER WHEN THEY USED TO SERVE LITTLE PRETZEL STICKS.
Guisewite

MY OLD BUDDY, ZACK, SPLIT UP WITH HIS WIFE AND ASKED IF HE COULD HANG OUT HERE.
THAT'LL BE NICE FOR YOU, IRVING.

NICE?! I'VE WAITED FOUR YEARS FOR THIS! MY DRINKING BUDDY'S BACK! MY CAROUSING BUDDY! ZACK!!

YEOOWCH!!

IS IT MY IMAGINATION, OR DID SOMEONE JUST BITE ME IN THE KNEE?
Guisewite

KAREN'S STILL FINISHING SCHOOL, SO IT JUST MADE SENSE FOR ME TO TAKE BECKY WHEN WE SPLIT UP.

YOU MEAN YOU AND BECKY ARE BOTH STAYING WITH IRVING?!
CLUNK!
CLUNK!

YEAH, I KNEW HE WOULDN'T MIND.
BONK BONK BONK!

BECKY'S A JOY TO HAVE AROUND.
Gulsewitz

ZACK, THIS IS A SINGLE'S BUILDING. I CAN'T HAVE A WAILING BABY HERE.
BECKY DOESN'T WAIL, DO YOU, HONEY?

ALL BABIES WAIL.
BECKY DOESN'T WAIL, DO YOU, SWEETIE?

I CANNOT HAVE A WAILING BABY STAYING IN MY APARTMENT!!!
COME ON, BUDDY. IT'S JUST FOR A FEW DAYS.

WAAAH!!
SHUT UP IN THERE!!
Gulsewitz

AFTER WORK I PICK BECKY UP AT DAY CARE AND COOK HER DINNER.
I GRAB SOME CARRY-OUT ON THE WAY HOME FROM WORK.
BABY

THEN WE PLAY GAMES, TALK ABOUT BECKY'S DAY, AND I PUT HER TO BED.
I PLOP DOWN ON THE COUCH AND WATCH TV.
BY

I WASH THE DISHES, DO THE LAUNDRY, PICK UP BECKY'S TOYS, AND HIT THE SACK!
I CALL SOME FRIENDS, READ THE SPORTS PAGE AND FALL ASLEEP DURING THE LATE SHOW!

OH, BOY, IS HE GETTING OLD!!
APARTMENTS 100 – 200
Gulsewitz

REMEMBER WHEN WE USED TO CRUISE THIS MALL AND CHECK OUT THE LADIES, IRVING?
DON'T TORTURE ME, ZACK.
SALE

WHAT WOMAN IS GOING TO LOOK AT A COUPLE OF GUYS WITH A 2-YEAR-OLD ?

A BABY ! A BABY !!

LET ME HOLD HER.
Guisewite

IT USED TO BE ALL A GUY NEEDED TO ATTRACT THE LADIES WAS A SPORTS CAR. I COULD HANDLE THAT.
APT 300

THEN PLANTS. A GUY WITH A FICUS BENJIMINA AND A $2,000 STEREO SYSTEM HAD IT MADE.

...BUT NOW I DON'T SEEM "WITH IT" UNLESS I HAVE A 2-YEAR-OLD AND A BRIEF-CASE FULL OF TOYS. CATHY, HOW AM I SUPPOSED TO DO THAT ??!
OH, IRVING...

PATHOS. THE UNIVERSAL CHARMER.
Guisewite

IN MODERN PARENTING, WE LEARN THAT A CHILD'S ACTIONS ARE ALWAYS MOTIVATED, IRVING.
SPLAT!

BECKY SENSES YOUR HOSTILITY TOWARDS HER, AND IS EXPRESSING HER FRUSTRATION BY THROWING FOOD AT YOU.

SPLAT!

I SEE BECKY'S IN THE FOOD-FLINGING STAGE.
ALSO A POSSIBILITY.
Guisewite

ALL RIGHT!!
ZACK'S IN THERE, CATHY. HE MUST BE WATCHING THE GAME !!
APT. 200

WAY TO GO!! HOORAY!
DARN! I'M MISSING IT! I GAVE HIM MY KEY.
APT. 200

YAHOO! BRAVO!!
LET ME IN, BUDDY! DID WE GET THE EXTRA POINT ??!
BAM BAM!

NO. BECKY USED HER POTTY SEAT!
I DON'T WANT TO GO IN JUST YET.

COOKIE. COOKIE PLEASE!

COOKIE! I WANT COOKIE PLEASE!

GIVE ME A COOKIE!!
IRVING, FOR HEAVEN'S SAKE. GIVE HER A COOKIE.

WOMEN INSTINCTIVELY KNOW HOW TO HANDLE CHILDREN.

ZACK AND BECKY MOVED INTO THEIR HOUSE TODAY, HUH?
YEAH...I DON'T KNOW HOW HE DOES IT, CATHY.

HE WAS MY BEST FRIEND IN SCHOOL--A WILD MAN--AND SUDDENLY HE'S TRANSFORMED INTO A TOTALLY DEVOTED FATHER OF A 2-YEAR-OLD.

THAT'S NOT SO HARD TO UNDERSTAND, IS IT, IRVING?
I GUESS NOT.

SOMETHING MUST HAPPEN TO YOUR BRAIN WHEN YOU HAVE CHEERIOS EMBEDDED IN YOUR FEET.

I BOUGHT A $90 DRESS FOR DINNER WITH IRVING TONIGHT.
FASHION MALL

I BOUGHT $20 PERFUME TO SMELL BEAUTIFUL FOR IRVING, AND $7 MASCARA SO I CAN GAZE MEANINGFULLY INTO IRVING'S EYES!

THIS YEAR, I'M GOING TO KEEP IRVING FASCINATED THROUGH FEBRUARY 14!!
YOU SPENT $117 TO KEEP IRVING FASCINATED THROUGH FEBRUARY 14??

I DIDN'T WANT TO WASTE THE 85¢ I SPENT ON HIS VALENTINE.
FASHION MALL
Guisewite

7:30... I STRIKE MY SULTRY, COME-HITHER POSE.

8:05... I STRIKE MY TOTALLY MIFFED POSE.

8:27... I STRIKE MY HOSTILITY POSE... NO. TOO MEAN... I STRIKE MY EMPATHY POSE... NO. TOO NICE... I STRIKE MY..
HI, CATHY. SORRY I'M SO LATE.

I'M NOT READY YET.
Guisewite

I LOOKED AT ALL THE VALENTINE'S DAY CARDS AND CANDY AND JEWELRY, HONEY...

...BUT NOTHING WAS LOVELY ENOUGH TO EXPRESS MY FEELINGS FOR YOU ON THIS MOST MEANINGFUL OCCASION.
OH.. WELL...

BONK!

AS WE GET OLDER, WE LEARN TO BE MORE DIRECT.
Guisewite

IRVING FLAKED-OUT ON VALENTINE'S DAY AGAIN? WHY DON'T YOU JUST SCREAM AT HIM, CATHY??
NO GOOD, ANDREA. I DID THAT LAST VALENTINE'S DAY.

HOW ABOUT THE SILENT TREATMENT??
NOPE. I DID THE SILENT TREATMENT IN 1977 AND 1980.

HOW ABOUT THE OLD GUILT-TORTURE APPROACH?!
NOPE. I USED THAT IN 1978, 1979 AND 1981.

THE LONGER YOU DATE SOMEONE, THE HARDER IT IS TO KEEP THINGS FRESH.

ECONOMY CLASS IS $592.
$592?! WHAT A RIP-OFF!
BUSINESS CLASS IS $745.
$745?! OUTRAGEOUS!
CATHY

AND FIRST CLASS IS $1186.
$1186?! ARE YOU OUT OF YOUR MIND?!
CATHY

GOOD MORNING. YOU'VE BEEN ASSIGNED THE CENTER SEAT, SURROUNDED BY SCREAMING BABIES AND AIR-SICK ADULTS.
FLIGHT 65

GROUCH CLASS.

AFTER EVERYTHING WE'VE BEEN THROUGH TOGETHER, I CAN'T BELIEVE YOU'D TURN ON ME LIKE THIS.
RECEPTION

I WAS ONLY GONE FOR TWO DAYS, AND LOOK AT YOU. YOU'RE A WRECK!
CATHY

SOMETIMES I WISH I'D NEVER MET YOU!!

MY DESK AND I JUST BROKE UP.

WHAT'S THIS DOING IN YOUR EXPENSE REPORT?

THAT'S MY GROCERY BILL FOR THE $52 OF FOOD THAT ROTTED IN MY REFRIGERATOR WHEN I WAS ON MY LAST STUPID BUSINESS TRIP!!

YOU WERE ONLY GONE ONE NIGHT, CATHY.

I HATE IT WHEN THE ACCOUNTING DEPARTMENT IS ON THEIR TOES.
ACCOUNTING DEPT.

WHAT COLOR ARE YOU GOING TO PAINT YOUR LIVING ROOM?
WHAT??
KISS
KISS
KISS
KISS
KISS

UM... THAT WAS SMALL TALK. IF YOU MAKE SMALL TALK, IT TAKES THE PRESSURE OFF A ROMANTIC MOMENT AND HELPS BOTH PEOPLE ENJOY THEMSELVES.

I'M KISSING YOU AND YOU'RE PLANNING SMALL TALK?? YOU'RE NUTS!!

SOMETIMES I GET THE FEELING MY MOTHER IS WRITING ALL THE MAGAZINE ARTICLES.

I DON'T KNOW, CATHY. I'D BETTER THINK ABOUT IT.
YOU HAVE THE OPINIONS OF TWO EXPERT WOMEN, MR. PINKLEY.
PINKLEY

YEAH, BUT LOOK AT THE NUMBERS SHE'S TALKING ABOUT.
MR. PINKLEY, YOU'RE ALWAYS TOO CONSERVATIVE AND THEN YOU COME WHINING TO ME.
PINKLEY

IF YOU'RE GOING TO BUY, BUY BIG! MAKE AN INVESTMENT THAT WILL COUNT!!!
PINKLEY

HOW DID YOU DO?
5 BOXES OF PEANUT BUTTER COOKIES... 4 BOXES OF THIN MINTS... AND 3 SANDWICH CREMES.
GIRL SCOUT COOKIES
CHARLENE
G.S. COOKIE

I WON'T BE IN TODAY, MR. PINKLEY. MY HAIR WON'T START.

WHERE ARE THEY?! WHERE ARE ALL THE SINGLE MEN?!!

STANDING ON YOUR BALCONY SCREAMING ISN'T GOING TO HELP, CATHY.

YOU'LL ONLY MEET SOMEONE NEW WHEN YOU JUST RELAX AND DO THE THINGS YOU NORMALLY DO.

THAT IS WHAT I NORMALLY DO.

I WILL NOT ASK CATHY ABOUT HER LOVE LIFE.
I WILL NOT YELL AT MOM FOR DROPPING BY UNINVITED.

I WILL NOT LECTURE CATHY ABOUT HER MESSY APARTMENT.
I WILL NOT BE ANNOYED BY THE 20 CLIPPINGS MOM BROUGHT OVER.

THE CONVERSATION REALLY SLOWS DOWN WHEN WE'RE CONTROLLING OURSELVES, DOESN'T IT?

I CAN'T STAND TO CALL THIS MAN, MR. PINKLEY.
I CAN'T, EITHER. LET'S PUT HIM OFF UNTIL MONDAY.

GOOD THINKING. THEN WE CAN PUSH THESE MEETINGS OFF UNTIL WEDNESDAY.
YES! THEN WE CAN AVOID THESE GUYS UNTIL THURSDAY!!

WAIT. THAT LEAVES US WITH 26 MEETINGS ON FRIDAY.
CAN'T YOU TWO EVER PLAN AHEAD?
WE ARE PLANNING AHEAD.

WE'RE CREATING NEXT WEEK'S DISASTERS.

SPINACH
CUCUMBERS
SPROUTS
TOMATOES
LETTUCE
MUSHROOMS
DRESSING
BROCCOLI
ZUCCHINI
FISH
LEMON
BUTTER
EGGS
SEASONINGS

ONE CHEESEBURGER AND A LARGE ORDER OF FRIES.

I NEED THE DOLLAR BACK THAT I LOANED YOU LAST WEEK, CHARLENE.
SORRY, CATHY. I LOANED IT TO JOE.

GET IT BACK, OKAY? I NEED IT FOR LUNCH.
I CAN'T. JOE LOANED IT TO MARY. MARY LOANED IT TO SUE.

SUE SENT IT TO TOLEDO TO PAY BACK HER BROTHER, WHO PAID BACK HIS ROOMMATE, WHO LOANED IT TO HIS GIRLFRIEND'S MOTHER IN FLORIDA.

A DOLLAR GOES A LOT FARTHER THAN IT USED TO.

HOW DOES THAT LEOTARD FIT ?
FINE. JUST FINE.
YOU DON'T NEED A LARGER SIZE ?
LARGER ? HA, HA! NO, THIS IS FINE.

OH GOOD! LET ME SEE IT ON YOU!

CRASH!
BONK!
CRASH!

WRONG COLOR.

HE TOLD ME HE LOVED ME AND THEN HE DIDN'T CALL FOR FIVE WEEKS...

FORGET HIM! SMASH HIS RECORDS! ERASE HIS TAPES!! DRIVE HIS MEMORY FROM YOUR MIND!!
WOMEN'S JACUZZI RULES

NOTHING CLEARS OUT A JACUZZI LIKE AN UNSOLICITED OPINION.

HELLO, CATHY, AND WHO'S THE LUCKY GUY ??
WHAT MAKES YOU THINK THERE'S A LUCKY GUY ?
RECEPTIONIST

EVERY TIME YOU GET INTERESTED IN SOMEONE NEW, YOU BUY A NEW PAIR OF SHOES.
RECEPTIONIST

YOU GOT THE TAUPE PUMPS WHEN YOU MET GRANT, REMEMBER ? THE OPEN-TOE BURGUNDY FOR DAVID... AND HUDSON'S ENTIRE FALL COLLECTION OF 2-TONES FOR YOUR REUNION WITH IRVING!

HOW EMBARRASSING. I'M WEARING MY HEART ON MY FEET.

HI THERE. I WAS ADMIRING YOU FROM ACROSS THE ROOM AND WONDERED IF I COULD BUY YOU A DRINK...

ME?? YES! I'VE WAITED ALL MY LIFE FOR A WOMAN TO ASK ME OUT! YES! BUY ME A DRINK! BUY ME DINNER!

BUY ME A CAR AND A HOUSE! YES! YA HA!! I AM ALL YOURS!!!

I CHANGED MY MIND.

YOU WALKED RIGHT UP AND ASKED ME OUT FOR A DRINK! I LOVE IT!!

OF COURSE, A "DRINK" IS THE IDEAL FIRST DATE. IF THE OTHER PERSON TURNS OUT TO BE OBNOXIOUS AND DISGUSTING, YOU'RE NOT STUCK WITH HIM FOR THE WHOLE EVENING.

WELL, I DON'T FIND YOU OBNOXIOUS AND DISGUSTING! SO HOW ABOUT IF WE STAY ON FOR DINNER??

I HATE QUESTIONS LIKE THAT.

MY GOAL IS TO MARRY AN AMBITIOUS CAREER WOMAN SO I CAN SPEND THE REST OF MY DAYS PERFECTING MY MUSCLE TONE.

SHE WILL WORK. I WILL JOG. SHE WILL COOK. I WILL LIFT WEIGHTS. SHE WILL CLEAN. I WILL ADMIRE MYSELF IN FULL-LENGTH MIRRORS!!

WHAT'S YOUR GOAL, CATHY?

MY GOAL IS TO REMEMBER WHAT YOU SAID LONG ENOUGH TO TELL MY GIRLFRIEND WHEN I GET HOME.

THAT GUY IS GORGEOUS, CATHY. WHY DID YOU TURN HIM DOWN FOR LUNCH?
WE HAVE NOTHING IN COMMON, CHARLENE.

I WORK 10 HOURS A DAY.
HE EXERCISES 10 HOURS A DAY.
I HAVE MEETINGS IN THE EVENING.
HE PLAYS RACQUETBALL.
I SLEEP ON THE WEEKEND.
HE RUNS MARATHONS.

WELL, I GUESS THAT ANSWERS THAT.
YEAH...

...WE ONLY HAVE 15 FREE MINUTES A WEEK. HOW MUCH IN COMMON DO WE NEED?

I RAN 6 MILES ON MONDAY!
I RAN FROM MY RELATIONSHIP WITH DAVID.

I RAN 7 MILES ON TUESDAY!
I RAN FROM MY RELATIONSHIP WITH GRANT.

I RAN 10 MILES TODAY!
I RAN FROM MY RELATIONSHIP WITH IRVING.

ARE YOU INTO RUNNING, CATHY?
YES.

I KNOW WHAT I WANT IN A RELATIONSHIP. I JUST HAVEN'T FOUND IT.
OH, BALONEY.

YOU EXPECT TOO MUCH, CATHY.

IN THE BIG PICTURE, ALL THAT MATTERS IS THAT YOU FIND SOMEONE WHO'S SENSIBLE, DEPENDABLE, PRACTICAL, VERSATILE, SOIL-RESISTANT, DRIP DRY...

YOU'RE DESCRIBING MY NAVY BLUE SKIRT, MOM.
SORRY. I GOT CARRIED AWAY.

HOW WAS THE BIG DATE LAST NIGHT, CATHY ?
MOM, I'M A GROWN, INDEPENDENT WOMAN.

I HARDLY THINK I NEED TO GIVE YOU A REPORT ON EVERY DATE.

CATHY, IF YOU'RE SO INDEPENDENT, WHY DID YOUR MOTHER EVEN KNOW YOU HAD A DATE LAST NIGHT ??

IT SLIPPED OUT WHEN SHE WAS BEGGING ME TO IRON AND HEM HER DRESS.

I'LL HAVE THE 7-SUMMER VEGETABLE SOUP AND A BUCKWHEAT MUFFIN.

I'LL HAVE THE NUT-AND-SEED PATTY AND A SMALL, UN-STRAINED CARROT JUICE.

I'M GOING TO NEED A LITTLE TIME TO MYSELF TONIGHT, BRIAN.
I UNDERSTAND, CATHY. YOU WANT SOME QUIET TIME TO REFLECT ON OUR NEW RELATIONSHIP.

I WANT TO GO EAT A BANANA SPLIT.

BRIAN HAS NO JOB, NO AMBITION, AND NO PERSONALITY. I'M DATING HIM STRICTLY FOR HIS LOOKS.
SO WHAT? YOU OWE IT TO YOURSELF, CATHY.

YOU OWE IT TO YOURSELF TO BUY A NEW OUTFIT FOR A GREAT-LOOKING GUY ! YOU OWE IT TO YOURSELF TO SPLURGE ON NEW COLOGNE FOR A GREAT-LOOKING GUY !!

AND YOU OWE IT TO YOURSELF TO TAKE THAT GREAT-LOOKING GUY OUT ON THE TOWN !!!
UP
DOWN

EVERY TIME YOU SAY, "I OWE IT TO MYSELF," I WIND UP OWING AMERICAN EXPRESS ANOTHER $50.
UP
DOWN

PHONE CALLS. THERE ARE TOO MANY PHONE CALLS.
RING RING RING!

HOW AM I SUPPOSED TO GET ANY WORK DONE WITH ALL THESE PHONE CALLS ??!!

YOU DIDN'T GET ANY PHONE CALLS THIS MORNING, CATHY.

I KNOW. I WAS LISTENING IN ON YOURS.

ON SUNDAY I TOLD IRVING I HAD TO STAY HOME AND DO THE LAUNDRY. BUT I REALLY WENT OUT WITH BRIAN.

ON MONDAY I TOLD IRVING I HAD TO PAY BILLS...I WENT OUT WITH BRIAN. ON TUESDAY I TOLD IRVING I HAD TO CLEAN... I WENT OUT WITH BRIAN.

TONIGHT IRVING'S COMING OVER. WHAT AM I GOING TO TELL HIM ??
WHY DO YOU HAVE TO TELL HIM ANYTHING, CATHY ?

I HAVE A FEELING HE'S GOING TO SUSPECT SOMETHING.
BILLS
BILLS
COOKIES

IRVING SAID, "HOW COULD YOU GO OUT WITH HIM ?!" I SAID, "OH DARLING, I WAS THINKING OF YOU EVERY MOMENT."
YOU DIDN'T SAY THAT, CATHY...

...YOU SCREAMED AT IRVING FOR SNOOPING INTO YOUR AFFAIRS AND HE STORMED OUT OF YOUR APARTMENT !
DIARY

I CAN'T BELIEVE YOU'RE SITTING THERE CHANGING A CONVERSATION YOU ALREADY HAD !!
DIARY

AS LONG AS I'M GOING TO LIVE IN THE PAST, I MIGHT AS WELL IMPROVE IT.
DIARY

WE ASSERTED OUR INDEPENDENCE IN TIGHT, STRAIGHT SKIRTS AND BUTTONED VESTS.

WE REAFFIRMED OUR FEMININITY IN MINI-SKIRTS AND SEE-THROUGH TOPS.

NOW WE ARE SALUTING OUR INDEPENDENT YET FEMININE HEALTHY BODIES IN DAZZLING LEOTARDS AND TIGHTS.

EVERY TIME WOMEN ENTER ANOTHER PHASE, THERE'S A WHOLE NEW CATEGORY OF CLOTHES I CAN'T GET INTO.

BUTTON UP YOUR BLOUSE, SWEETIE. YOU DON'T WANT TO GIVE THE WRONG IMPRESSION.
OH, FOR HEAVEN'S SAKE, MOTHER. THIS IS 1983.

NEVER BE PUSHY. PUSHY WOMEN ARE VERY UNATTRACTIVE.
MOM, THIS IS BUSINESS. I HAVE TO BE PUSHY TO GET AHEAD.

PUT THE ROLL DOWN, DEAR. YOU HAVE POTATOES COMING WITH YOUR MEAL.
THERE IS NOTHING WRONG WITH ONE ROLL.

CATHY! I CAN'T BELIEVE A WHOLE WEEK HAS SLIPPED BY SINCE I TALKED TO YOU!
NEITHER CAN I, MOM...

SHAMPOO I TRIED ONCE AND HATED... COLOGNE I'VE GOTTEN SICK OF... FACE CREAM THAT DIDN'T WORK...

MAKEUP THAT'S THE WRONG COLOR... HAIR CLIPS THAT WON'T STAY IN MY HAIR... BUBBLE BATH THAT I'M ALLERGIC TO...

MY BATHROOM CUPBOARDS ARE FILLED WITH THINGS I WILL NEVER USE, FORCING ME TO THROW THE THINGS I DO USE ALL OVER THE COUNTER!

THE FAMILY TRADITION LIVES ON!!

I VOTE FOR BRIAN. IF CATHY TURNS HIM DOWN AGAIN, HE'LL LOSE ALL INTEREST.
SO WHAT? SHE'S BETTER OFF READING A BORING BOOK TONIGHT.

I VOTE FOR IRVING.
YOU WOULD. YOU'RE JUST LIKE HIM. PUT ME DOWN FOR BRIAN.
BRIAN. HAH! I'LL...

WHAT IS THE MATTER WITH YOU PEOPLE?? YOU'VE JUST WASTED 15 MINUTES TRYING TO MAKE DECISIONS ABOUT MY LOVE LIFE!!

...SORRY TO KEEP YOU WAITING, BRIAN. THEY USUALLY VOTE FASTER THAN THIS.

BRIAN TOOK ME OUT FOR A SALAD.

WE MET FOR A FRUIT PLATE FOR LUNCH...HE BEGGED ME TO SPLIT A STRAWBERRY YOGURT AFTER WORK...

NOW HE WANTS ME TO COME TO HIS PLACE FOR STEAMED EGGPLANT AND BROCCOLI JUICE.

CATHY, IF YOU DON'T LIKE HIM, WHY DON'T YOU JUST TELL HIM NO??
I CAN'T. I'M STARTING TO LOSE WEIGHT.

WHY DIDN'T YOU JUST TELL ME YOU WERE GOING OUT WITH SOMEONE ELSE?
I DIDN'T WANT TO HURT YOU, IRVING.

YOU WOULD HAVE GOTTEN MAD AND HELD IT AGAINST ME FOR THE NEXT YEAR.

THAT WOULD HAVE HURT YOU, NOT ME, CATHY.
..THEN I WOULD HAVE GOTTEN FED UP AND HIT YOU. THAT WOULD HAVE HURT YOU.

...SO MUCH FOR THE OLD "PLANNING AHEAD" APPROACH.

CAN I GET YOU ANYTHING ELSE ?
YES. I WANT ANSWERS.

I WANT TO KNOW WHAT GOES ON INSIDE THE MALE BRAIN THAT CAN MAKE ONE MAN SO CHARMING AND SO VAGUE AT THE SAME TIME ??

WHAT IS IT MEN WANT AND WHY DON'T THEY JUST SAY IT INSTEAD OF PUTTING US THROUGH THIS TORTURE GUESSING GAME THAT DESTROYS OUR SELF-CONFIDENCE AND PERSONALITIES?!

MOVE OVER.

I WISH I'D MET YOU BEFORE, CATHY.
YOU WOULDN'T HAVE LIKED ME BEFORE, BRIAN. I HAD NO SELF-ESTEEM.

I USED TO COOK FOR MY DATE, CLEAN FOR MY DATE, IRON FOR MY DATE, DO WHAT MY DATE WANTED TO DO, THINK THE WAY MY DATE THOUGHT...

I USED TO LIVE MY WHOLE LIFE FOR THE PERSON I WAS DATING!!

NOW I REALLY WISH I'D MET YOU BEFORE.

MILK, $2.14 A HALF GALLON... COFFEE CREAM, 59¢ A PINT... ORANGE JUICE, $1.98 A QUART...
MILK

TOMATO JUICE, 99¢ A CAN... DIET POP, $2.19 A SIX-PACK ... MINERAL WATER, $1.03 A BOTTLE...

... FOR A GRAND TOTAL OF $32.18.
MILK

HI, CATHY. WHERE HAVE YOU BEEN?
I JUST LIQUIDATED MY ASSETS.
TOMATO JUICE

AACK! THE CLIENT WANTS A COMPLETE REVISION IN ONE HOUR, CATHY!

EMERGENCY! CHANGE DIRECTION! THE REVISION OF THE REVISION IS DUE IN 20 MINUTES!!

CANCEL THE WHOLE PROJECT! THE CLIENT WANTS IT THE WAY IT WAS IN THE FIRST PLACE!!

SOME DAYS YOU'RE HOT.
Guisewite

BRIAN, I ONLY WENT OUT WITH YOU BECAUSE I NEEDED TO BOOST MY EGO IN THE MOST SUPERFICIAL WAY.
NUMERO UNO

I NEEDED TO REMIND MYSELF WHAT IT WAS LIKE TO DATE AN EGOMANIAC SO I WON'T BE TEMPTED BY A CUTE FACE IN THE FUTURE.
NUMERO UNO

AND I NEEDED TO PRACTICE DEALING FRANKLY AND HONESTLY WITH SOMEONE I DON'T ACTUALLY LIKE MUCH.
NUMERO UNO

DO YOU UNDERSTAND WHAT I'M SAYING, BRIAN?
YOU NEED ME!!
NUMERO UNO
Guisewite

I HOPE WE CAN STILL BE FRIENDS, CATHY.
FRIENDS AS IN, "I WILL ALWAYS LOVE YOU"... OR FRIENDS AS IN, "WE'LL STAY IN TOUCH UNTIL YOU RETURN MY ALBUMS"?

FRIENDS AS IN, "I'LL CALL IF I DON'T MEET SOMEONE BETTER"... FRIENDS AS IN, "PLEASE DON'T SAY MEAN THINGS ABOUT ME TO YOUR SWEET MOTHER"...

...OR FRIENDS AS IN, "I NEVER WANT TO SEE YOUR DISGUSTING FACE AGAIN"?

ONE MIND, ONE THOUSAND MISINTERPRETATIONS.
Guisewite

OH, POOR BABY! BRIAN DUMPED YOU!! HAVE SOME BROWNIES!!
BRIAN DIDN'T DUMP ME, MOM.

BRIAN DIDN'T DUMP YOU??

BRIAN MIGHT HAVE DUMPED ME SOMETIME IN THE FUTURE.
BRIAN MIGHT HAVE DUMPED YOU.

OH, POOR BABY! HAVE SOME BROWNIES!!
...THE THINGS I'LL DO FOR CHOCOLATE....

HI. MAY I BORROW A PEN?
I DON'T HAVE ONE. BUT I HAVE A BRAN MUFFIN AND A MINI-TOOL-KIT WITH 6 BREATH MINTS STUCK ON IT.

I HAVE 3 DEAD BATTERIES, HALF A YOGURT, 14 FRENCH FRIES AND A STONES TAPE!
I HAVE 35 PIECES OF UNWRAPPED SUGARLESS GUM, A TUBE OF TOOTH-PASTE WITH NO TOP, AND THE STOCK MARKET!

MAY I HELP YOU, LADIES?

WE DON'T WANT ANYTHING ANYMORE.

I THOUGHT YOU'D BE OUT WITH THAT BEAN SPROUT TONIGHT, CATHY.
BRIAN IS HISTORY, IRVING.

OH YEAH?
HE'S GONE! HE'S OUT OF MY LIFE! HE IS HISTORY!

HI, CUTIE.

HISTORY JUST REPEATED ITSELF.

HOW CAN YOU DEVELOP FILM IN AN HOUR? THE OTHER PLACES TAKE 7 DAYS.
SIMPLE. ONLY 3 OF US WORK HERE.
ONE HOUR
ONE HOU DEVELOP

THEREFORE, THERE ARE ONLY 3 OF US TO TAKE TURNS GAWKING AND GIGGLING OVER THE PICTURES YOU TOOK.
ONE

THE OTHER PLACES EMPLOY LOTS OF PEOPLE...SO, NATURALLY, IT TAKES THE FULL 7 DAYS BEFORE YOUR PICTURES CAN BE PASSED AROUND AND STARED AT BY EVERYONE!!
ONE

DID YOU GET OUR PICTURES BACK, CATHY?
OOPS. I FORGOT TO TAKE THE FILM IN.
Guisewite

I DO NOT THINK "WELCOME TO THE ZOO" IS AN APPROPRIATE WALL PLAQUE FOR THE RECEPTION AREA, CHARLENE.
WELCOME TO THE ZOO

YOU'RE THE FIRST ONE PEOPLE ENCOUNTER HERE. THUS, IT'S YOUR JOB TO PROPERLY COMMUNICATE THE TONE OF OUR WHOLE OFFICE.

RIP
RIP
RIP

MUCH BETTER.
WELCOME TO THE FUNNY FARM
Guisewite

I WAS HALFWAY THROUGH THE ARGUS PROJECT WHEN I HAD TO START RETURNING SOME CALLS...I WAS HALFWAY THROUGH THE CALLS WHEN I HAD TO START WORKING ON MY TAXES...

I WAS HALFWAY THROUGH THE TAXES WHEN I HAD TO START DOING LAUNDRY...I WAS HALFWAY THROUGH THE LAUNDRY WHEN I HAD TO START PAYING BILLS...

I'M SICK OF COMPETING WITH YOUR WHOLE LIFE FOR A FEW MINUTES OF YOUR TIME. WE'RE THROUGH, CATHY!
I CAN'T BELIEVE IT.

THAT'S THE FIRST THING I'VE FINISHED ALL WEEK.
Guisewite

MY FRIEND FLO'S DAUGHTER'S EX-ROOMMATE SAW CATHY HAVING DINNER WITH IRVING TONIGHT AND CATHY DID NOT LOOK HAPPY.

FLO CALLED THE JOHNSTON FAMILY, WHO ALERTED LOUISE, WHO CALLED MARTHA, WHO CALLED JOAN, WHO WIRED SUSAN, WHO FINALLY TRACKED ME DOWN AT THE MARKET...
TRASH
101

CATHY, SWEETIE...TELL YOUR MOTHER WHAT'S WRONG !!
MOM ! HOW DID YOU KNOW ??

SOME DAYS MOTHERLY INTUITION TAKES MORE OF US THAN OTHERS.

WHAT SHOULD I SAY IF IRVING ASKS ME OUT ?
IF HE ASKS YOU OUT FOR FRIDAY NIGHT, IT MEANS YOU'RE SECOND CHOICE. TELL HIM NO.

IF HE ASKS YOU OUT FOR SATURDAY NIGHT, IT MEANS HE PROBABLY JUST BROKE UP WITH SOMEONE AND WILL TRY TO MOLD YOU INTO HIS EX-GIRLFRIEND. TELL HIM NO.

ALL THE "WINNERS" OF FRIDAY AND SATURDAY NIGHT GET DISPLAYED AT SUNDAY BRUNCH. IF HE ASKS YOU OUT FOR SUNDAY BRUNCH, TELL HIM NO !

...SUDDENLY, I'M STARTING TO WISH IT WAS MONDAY.

ANGER EVENTUALLY PASSES. FRUSTRATION GOES AWAY. EVEN LOVE CAN DISAPPEAR.

WHY IS IT THAT ONLY EMBARRASSMENT STAYS EXACTLY AS INTENSE FIVE YEARS LATER AS IT WAS THE MOMENT YOU WERE FIRST EMBARRASSED ABOUT SOMETHING ??!

...AND WHY DO I KEEP RE-PROVING THAT THEORY ?

IRVING, WE WERE JUST GETTING CLOSE AND THEN - POOF! - YOU DISAPPEARED AGAIN.

WHAT'S HIS EXCUSE THIS TIME, CATHY?

HE WANTS TO KEEP THE MAGIC IN OUR RELATIONSHIP.

IRVING LOVES YOU, CATHY.
REALLY? YOU REALLY THINK SO?
HE'S CRAZY ABOUT YOU!
MAYBE HE IS CRAZY ABOUT ME!

HE CAN'T LIVE ANOTHER MOMENT WITHOUT YOU!!
HE CAN'T LIVE ANOTHER MOMENT WITHOUT ME!!

...AND MEN WONDER WHY WE LIKE SPENDING TIME WITH OUR GIRLFRIENDS.

FOOD... LOVE...

MOTHER... CAREER...

LIVE EVERY DAY TO THE FULLEST.

PARTAKE OF THE FOUR BASIC GUILT GROUPS.